IRAN
SINCE THE REVOLUTION

Internal Dynamics,
Regional Conflict,
and the Superpowers

Edited by
Barry M. Rosen

SOCIAL SCIENCE MONOGRAPHS, BOULDER

DISTRIBUTED BY COLUMBIA UNIVERSITY PRESS, NEW YORK

1985

Brooklyn College Studies on Society in Change
No. 47
Editor-in-Chief
Béla K. Király

To Barbara, Alexander, and Ariana

Table of Contents

III. Iran and the Strategic
Rivalry in the Region

List of Maps

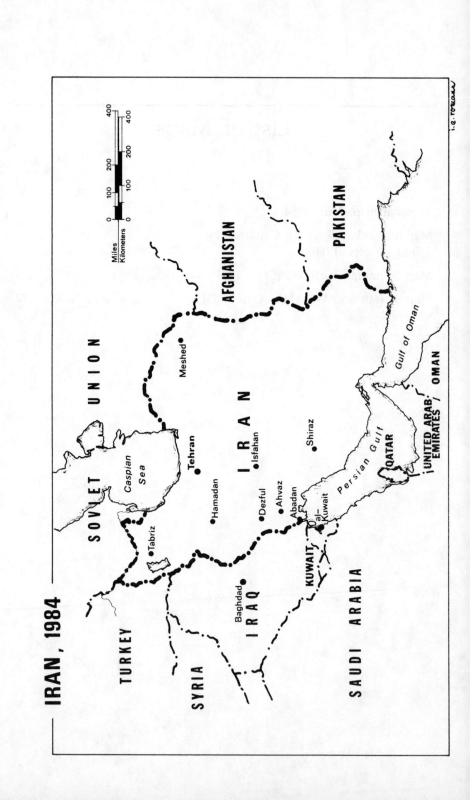

IRAN, 1984

Preface

This volume was originally conceived as part of a conference organized by the editor at Brooklyn College in the spring of 1983. Sponsored by the Brooklyn College Humanities Institute and funded by the Ford Foundation, the conference was the first college- or university-sponsored program in the United States on Iran since the conclusion of the hostage crisis. This is a remarkable fact when juxtaposed with A. M. Rosenthal's description of the United States during those 444 days, in which Americans were "moved, angered, frustrated, and quite full of questions about what happened, what went wrong, . . . [and] what was going on."

The conference and this volume focus on definite aspects of what is going on: the ideology of the Islamic Republic of Iran and its new parameters in relations with its neighbors and the superpowers. Ideology as a motive force in Iran is explored in the context of Islamic revivalism, the historical evolution of the doctrine of the Hidden Imam, and revolutionary graphics as political propaganda. The populist spirit of that ideology, expressed in announcements that "everything is reversed now, and the people who were on the bottom are on top" is played out in chapters on the Iran-Iraq War, Saudi attitudes toward the Islamic Revolution, and the historical Iran-Israel relationship. The strategic implications of the Khomeini world view that the great powers "are all worse than each other" and the question of how the United States and the Soviet Union interact with an unconventional Iran are the subjects of the concluding section of the volume.

I feel fortunate to have had Shahrough Akhavi write the introduction and Richard Cottam, Bill Hanaway, and Farhad Kazemi serve as members of the editorial board. I would like to thank all who participated in the original planning of the conference, especially Jiman Tagavi, and those whose scholarship enhanced the final result of that endeavor. Those of us who have been a part of the project from the very start are particularly indebted to the Ford Foundation and Béla K. Király and Jonathan A. Chanis of the Brooklyn College Program on Society in Change for their confidence and support. Finally, I am grateful to Brooklyn College President Robert L. Hess for his personal interest in this volume.

Barry M. Rosen
Brooklyn College
February 1984

SHAHROUGH AKHAVI

Introduction:
Ideology and the
Iranian Revolution

The following essays underscore in one way or another the importance
of ideology in contemporary politics. Developments in Iran since 1978
indicate how wrong certain social scientists were when, in the late 1950s,
they claimed that our age had seen "the end of ideology."[1] This is not,
of course, to say that ideas determine behavior. Instead, it would be
more accurate to say that ideas and behavior have mutually reinforcing
effects. Richard Cottam, for example, makes a plausible argument for
viewing Khomeini as a true believer who has no action program but
is proud of possessing an ideology. Yet, he also shows how politically
pragmatic the Iranian leadership is when it comes to finding allies, as
is evident in its support of the secularist government of Syrian President
Hafez al-Asad despite the latter's brutal suppression of Muslim fundamentalist protest in Hama in 1982. Those who would argue that this
incident disposes of the allegation that the Iranians are motivated by
ideology must then explain why they have made so many enemies of
surrounding states by insisting on their particular version of Islamic
salvation. It would perhaps be fruitful to view ideological variables not
as determining actual behavior but as providing the faithful with standards
for ruling out certain courses of action. From this point of view it
becomes clearer why the Iranian leaders reject the idea of good relations
with the Soviet Union as long as that country's troops occupy Afghanistan
(see the chapters by Cottam, Khalilzad, and Rubin) but also why the
Afghan question has not led Tehran to build anti-Soviet coalitions.

To concede the relevance of ideology in politics, then, it is unnecessary
to insist on 100 percent consistency on the part of the social actors
under investigation. If we were to adopt such a strict standard we
would have to view all behavior across all political systems and times
as opportunistic, ideology entering the picture merely as ex post facto
rationalization. Farhad Kazemi, for example, points out that ideological

commitments led the revolutionary regime to break relations with Israel at the outset, but he also shows that it bought weapons indirectly from the Israelis in the course of the war with Iraq. How serious, one might ask, were those commitments? Tactical accommodations such as this do not, however, alter the basic strategically hostile orientation of the Iranian regime toward Israel. Any ideological system must be flexible enough to overcome threats to its survival. Lenin is reported to have faced this dilemma at one point early in the Soviet revolution; unable to be present at a meeting of the leadership that had to decide whether to obtain weapons from the British and the French, he sent it the following message: "Please register my vote in favor of taking potatoes and arms from the Anglo-French imperialist brigands."[2] In the Iranian case, Shi'ite Islamic values permit resort to expediency (*taqiyya*) when the community is in danger of collapse. It is also permissible to invoke "secondary principles" (*qava'ed thanaviyya*) such as "collective interests" if adherence to primary principles (e.g., the paramountcy of property ownership) could endanger the community. Thus the adoption of solutions that are, strictly speaking, ideologically "out of bounds" is not deceitful. The ideological prism of the Iranian revolutionaries provides general principles and orientations so basic that all the authors writing on foreign-policy issues in this volume (Quandt, Tagavi, Kazemi, Cottam, Khalilzad, and Rubin) have seen fit to indicate their significance.

Jiman Tagavi, while basically presenting a factual exposition, nonetheless reminds us that ideological factors have been important in the course of the Iran-Iraq War and in the larger issue of regime legitimacy. Barry Rubin, examining U.S.-Iranian relations, devotes half his essay to internal Iranian developments and notes the anomaly that ideological fervor is so high that it has led to a situation in which "normal" politics—deterrence, negotiations, quid pro quo bargaining—do not "work." Richard Cottam takes this one step farther and argues that, while Iranian regimes in the past could ill afford poor relations with the two major foreign powers competing to influence Iranian politics and policies, the clerical regime has confounded this historical pattern by adopting hostile attitudes and conduct toward both. Zalmay Khalilzad notes that the Soviet Union has been unable to make inroads in Iran because of its perception by the clerics in Iran as "satanic." William Quandt shows that the Saudi Arabian elite has felt both angry and fearful over Iranian threats to export the revolution. Ironically, the Saudis have historically regarded themselves as the supremely "Islamic" leaders of the area, but in any case their reaction to events across the Gulf suggests the powerful role played by individuals obsessed with a moral vision of the world. Farhad Kazemi concludes that the Iranian regime's "all-out drive toward Islamization of the social order" has entrained major difficulties for the country's Jewish community. Iranian Jews are seen as at least potential, if not actual, agents of the Zionist state, a state that has encroached on Muslim territory and must therefore be treated as an enemy.

I have so far avoided issues of definition, but a definition of ideology is required in the interest of clarity. An ideology is a system of beliefs about politics and society whereby ideas are used as weapons to establish, defend, and promote interests. An ideology, as Edward Shils once indicated,[3] is distinct from an attitude, outlook, creed, or *Weltanschauung* on a number of dimensions: (1) explicitness of articulation of concepts; (2) extent of internal integration of the basic concepts with one another and with principles deducible from them; (3) degree of authoritativeness of formulation of doctrines; (4) amount of consensus demanded of adherents; (5) extent to which behavior is expected to reflect beliefs; (6) degree of susceptibility to foreign ideas; (7) depth of emotional attachment of adherents; (8) strength of association with a social movement or corporate organization. Those belief systems are ideologies that can be shown to be more explicit, more integrated, more authoritative, more unquestioned, more demanding of behavioral consistency, more closed to rival views, more emotionally compelling, and more strongly associated with a movement or corporate form. Ideologies, moreover, purport to criticize the past, explain the present, and point to, if not predict, the future order of things.

In this volume, the essays by Mangol Bayat, Nikki Keddie, and William Hanaway suggest that Khomeini's *velayat-e faqih* (governance by the supreme cleric) within the Shi'ite paradigm qualifies as an ideology every bit as much as does, say, Lenin's "democratic centralism" within the Marxist paradigm. Of course, Khomeini's ideology has its Shi'ite opponents, just as Lenin's has had contenders within the Marxist tradition. Khomeini's Shi'ite rivals include distinguished *mojtaheds*, the guerrilla group known as the Mojahedin-e Khalq, nonclerical but religious-minded nationalists, disaffected bazaaris, and certain ethnolinguistic minorities, to name but a few. The list of Lenin's Marxist rivals was also long: the "legal Marxists," the "economists," the Mensheviks, the "God Builders," the "Liberation of Laborists," the Socialist Revolutionaries, etc.

If Khomeini is a radical innovator within the Shi'ite tradition, as Bayat cogently argues, this does not mean that he is not a valid contributor to its theory of politics and authority. The roots of *velayat-e faqih* may go no deeper than the nineteenth century, but from now on any analyst of Shi'ite doctrine will have to account for it as an element of that doctrine. Similarly, the Constitutional Revolution of 1905–11 made Mohammad Hosain Na'ini's treatise *Tanbih al-Omma va Tanzih al-Mella* (1909) an important contribution to the development of Shi'ite doctrine.

Na'ini used the very general principle of *al-amr be 'l-ma'ruf va al-nahy 'an al-monkar* (commanding the good and enjoining from evil) as the theoretical underpinning for an adequate defense of constitutional limitations on the power of secular rulers. While such general principles as this are not as compelling as textual specification (*nass*) in so crucial an area as clerical rule or leadership in politics,[4] one hardly hesitates to grant Na'ini's work doctrinal validity for Shi'ite theory. It may well be that Khomeini's *velayat-e faqih* will play a similar role.

As Bayat shows, Shi'ite tradition and doctrine have urged the ulama to take collective leadership roles in society but left actual rule—both spiritual and secular—to the Hidden Imam. *Velayat-e faqih* counters with the notion of social responsibility and admonishes that passive anticipation of the Imam's return amounts to complicity in secular rulers' wrongdoing, especially in the matter of extending the jurisdiction of secular (*'orf*) at the expense of religious (*shar'*) law. Khomeini's discourse since 1963, in fact, has contained symbols potent enough ultimately to generate massive popular collective protest. In fact, as Nikki Keddie says, the Iranian Revolution is probably the only modern example of a religious revivalist movement that has succeeded in taking power. Whatever else the revolution has in common with previous revivalist movements, it is in some respects sui generis. Tactical power is accorded the Iranian Shi'ite clergy (but not their Sunni colleagues) as a result of (1) the messianic principles of the doctrine of the Imamate; (2) the financial autonomy of the clergy; (3) the vindication of the high clergy's right to exercise independent judgment; and (4) the obligation of the faithful to follow the teachings of a living *mojtahed* in matters of ritual and law. Most of these elements have to do with the impact of ideas, and this is yet another level of exemplification of the importance of Shi'ite ideas, values, perceptions, and symbols for social action.[5] In this connection, William Hanaway's conclusion is pertinent: the specifically Iranian Islamic elements of this revolution have been of greater significance to its participants than its more general Third World aspects. Hanaway, of course, is not saying that such Third World revolutions (those of Mexico, China, Vietnam, Algeria, and Cuba come to mind) were not consequential in ideological terms. He is, however, strongly implying that Iranians prefer Shi'ite symbolism to symbolism that has more universal meaning in world revolutionary experience in this century. True, this is a matter of poster art, but such depictions of revolutionary praxis have a powerful way of shaping moral visions even as they reflect them.

The authors of these essays seem agreed that at the very least Khomeini's departure from the scene will be necessary before the regime begins behaving "less ideologically," as it were. Empirical evidence from the historical record tends to support this view, as charismatic leaders and their ideological commitments are often replaced by managerial ones with technocratic and pragmatic values. It may be, however, that Iranian politics will not easily return to an essentially pragmatic course in the post-Khomeini era. Shi'ism, however interpreted, has long been an authentic element of this country's culture, and the ideology of Shi'ites will continue to motivate their social action. The sociological theory of religion to the contrary notwithstanding, Iranian society is not going through a "crisis of theology" in the sense of widespread abandonment of religion and profound questioning of its relevance. Nor, it needs to be said, was this the case in the Pahlavi period. Weberian sociology of religion suggests that rationalization leads to pluralism, industrialization, and, inevitably, secularization.[6] But rationalization in Iranian society in the Pahlavi period bifurcated its culture in such a way that its Shi'ite elements, however attenuated, were never marginalized for what we now know was the majority of the population.

Because the Iranian upheaval seems above all to be a cultural revolution, it stands to reason that its ideological underpinnings have received a great deal of reinforcement in the last five years. Even after Khomeini the clergy's active role in political life will not easily be denied. In the event that the military assumes power, for example, it will likely need to enter into a coalition with some faction of the currently contending clerical forces. It is possible, perhaps even probable, that this faction will not be associated with the Islamic Republican Party (IRP), the creation of the Khomeini clergy, but Shi'ism as ideology will likely continue to exercise significant influence in Iranian politics.

Does this mean that doctrinal tenets will cause Iranians to behave in prescribed ways? Hardly, for two reasons: First, complex doctrinal concepts are not easily understood by most people in a position to act politically. Secondly, even if such concepts did underlie the collective behavior of individuals, that behavior would probably not conform to any pattern somehow prescribed in advance. If this is conceded, however, how can one argue that ideology will continue to be relevant in the dynamics of Iranian politics? Simply put, the answer is that the values in Shi'ite cultural traditions—oppression, martyrdom, salvation, piety, and others—are understandable and meaningful. Such arcane arguments as that problems of authority in the absence of the requirement of the oath of allegiance to the Hidden Imam cannot be resolved until his return are not readily followed by rank-and-file believers. It is feasible, however, to fashion an exoteric doctrine out of the values just mentioned while the arcane arguments remain the esoteric core issues. The latter, though crucial for the existence of the ideology, do not have to be readily understood by most people.

Now, if in the post-Khomeini era a faction of the clergy that disagrees with *velayat-e faqih* becomes influential, it can still base its political action upon Shi'ite concepts of authority. It might, for example, opt for administrative oversight (*vesaya*) of secular rule by the clerics. While not assuming executive posts, the clergy would constitute a committee empowered to invalidate laws and behavior considered against the strictures of Shi'ism. Under this arrangement, the presumption would be that rule is in the hands of others but on the sufferance of the clergy. Instead of the ideology of *velayat-e faqih*, one would have the ideology of *vesayat-e faqih*.

To make the point clearer, it may be helpful to draw an analogy to politics elsewhere. In the Soviet Union after the revolution of 1917, most workers and peasants and probably even certain Bolshevik leaders could not be said to have understood Marx's discussion of the labor theory of value, with its elements of use value, exchange value, and the "rising organic composition of capital." But they certainly did appear to be inspired by aspects of Marxism-Leninism that focused on class conflict in society. In the Iranian case, the need for a proof of God's existence incarnate in the Imam as the basis of the Shi'ite view of salvation may be too recondite for the popular mind, but the violation of the Imam's justice by tyrants is readily appreciated.

As we have seen, Shils says that an ideology tends to be closely associated wtih a social movement or corporate form. How does *velayat-e faqih* measure up on this dimension? To answer this question, the analyst will focus on two institutions, one of which is the IRP. By all accounts, the IRP is far from being the "organizational weapon," in Selznick's terms, that the Communist party was in the Soviet Union at a comparable point in its revolution. This does not, however, mean that, measured on this dimension, Khomeini's *velayat-e faqih* is not an ideology. In the first place, the categories are not meant as either-or dichotomies. Additionally, that the IRP is not a credible revolutionary institution when compared with the Soviet Communist party may simply mean that the major vehicle of revolutionary mobilization and action does not have to be a political party. In the Iranian case, most people would agree that it is an informal institution, the *emam-e jom'a* (Friday mosque leaders)/preacher network, that plays this role. Although informally constituted, it has considerable resources, including the financial support of the pro-Khomeini top clergy and the theological seminaries, which provide the cadres for it. With its lines of communication to the revolutionary guards and committees, the network services primarily the urban poor, the chief social force of the revolution. Participation in the network is a more reliable predictor of membership in the party than party membership is a predictor of participation in the network.

Velayat-e faqih thus constitutes the ideology of Khomeini Shi'ism. It is an ideology that is explicit in identifying the problems of society, although it is admittedly less specific on how to solve them. It is an ideology that is deducible from such central concepts of Imamite Shi'ism as monotheism, prophecy, salvation, the Islamic community (*omma*), the Imamate, *velayat* (the Imam's rule), the occultation of the Imam, the general agency (*al-vekalat al-'amma*) of religious leaders during the Imam's occultation, anticipation of the Imam's return (*entezar*), and martyrdom.

The authoritativeness of this ideology is claimed to be of the very highest, but there are strong disagreements, even today, among the top clergymen over the question of whether it is justified by classical doctrine. The best that can be said for *velayat-e faqih* by those seeking supreme authoritative sanction for it in the great classical works of Shi'ite *hadith* (sayings attributed to the prophet and the imams) is that these works do not specifically rule it out. At the same time, Khomeini's arguments are considered by many *mojtaheds* to be thin from the point of view of scholarship. Nonetheless, his authority was strong enough to silence clerical critics in the early part of the revolution, and even now, when it is abundantly clear that the regime has resorted to coercion to suppress dissent, many non-IRP clerics probably still view Khomeini as an authentic *marja'-e taqlid* (a title reserved for a handful of the eminent *mojtaheds* of a particular historical period).

The high degree of consensus demanded of this ideology's followers, as well as the requirement that their behavior conform to the dictates of the ideology, is evident in the war with Iraq. The concomitant high level of emotional commitment to the cause among the urban poor and the so-called *basij-e enqelabi* (the revolutionary wave mobilized and sent to the front) has been well described in the international media.

Yet, withal, *velayat-e faqih* faces serious problems. In fact, some of the analytical categories adumbrated in the preceding discussion are "at war" with one another, so to speak. This is a dilemma virtually all ideologies seem to contend with. Their very strength is a weakness. The more closed an ideology becomes to alternatives, the more it risks dogmatism, which ultimately leads to a loss of flexibility and adaptability. Furthermore, at a certain point authoritativeness of formulation shades into authoritarianism in formulation. The sustained high levels of affective attachment become perverted into rigid fanaticism or end in emotional burnout. Either way, the ideology becomes increasingly formalistic and irrelevant to changing circumstances. Diminishing returns are reached at the point when consensus is exacted at the expense of creativity and initiative. As the categories are carried to their logical conclusion by the ideological die-hards, the ideology comes to suffer an odd combination of entropy and hypertrophy: excessive growth in certain of its aspects leads to the degradation of the system.

It is possible to perceive these problems in current domestic Iranian politics. According to the ideology, mass mobilization is essential for validating and revalidating the worth of the revolutionary experience in the face of God's placing His trusts in the people, but fewer people are now being politically mobilized for parades, referenda, etc. This is to be expected, since it is unrealistic to anticipate continued perfervid mobilization of the people without respite, but the current apathy seems more widespread than the passage of time would normally produce. The slogans of the revolution, such as *na sharqi, na gharbi, faqat jomhuri-ye eslami* ("Neither Eastern nor Western, just an Islamic Republic") must now make room for ironic ones such as *ya barq-e da'em, ya shah-e kha'en* ("Either give us uninterrupted electricity or give us back the traitorous shah").

As Rubin points out, factional conflict exists within the ruling clergy. Whether it is due exclusively to the emergence of a Maktabi-Hojjatiyya split or whether the Maktabis (those more unequivocally in favor of *velayat-e faqih*) are more seriously divided than their rhetoric suggests, the fact is that factionalism is a serious problem in Iranian politics and has led Khomeini to make repeated calls for unity. The prevailing group, the one Keddie terms the "conservatives," is powerful enough to have blocked the passage of a land law containing strong redistribution provisions. It has also vetoed labor legislation aimed at giving workers a measure of autonomy through workers' councils. It would be misleading to argue that only those clergymen who are not Maktabis have managed to form such effective blocking coalitions, since it could then be asked why Khomeini does not put an end to their recalcitrance. The truth is that support for the conservative position must exist among the Maktabis themselves. So far, however, public attacks upon rivals have been confined to oblique references to "certain people" who are behaving in allegedly antirevolutionary ways. It should also be noted that on a number of issues Khomeini himself will not take a clear-cut stand, either because he has not yet made up his mind or because he perceives that the position he favors does not have enough support or, finally, because he wants to prevent the crystallization of positions in an effort to promote "permanent revolution."

Ideological militance in foreign affairs also threatens *velayat-e faqih* with entropy/hypertrophy. The regime probably lost more than it gained from any rational-calculus/means-ends perspective in the matter of the American hostages. It has given up considerable international prestige and finds itself in adversary relations with a wide array of nations. Friendly relations with North Korea are probably not something most politically conscious Iranians place high on their list of priorities. It is true that the hostage affair humiliated the American government, but this has been more of a short-term gain in view of the resulting loss of resources and revenues from the ensuing embargo on trade and freezing of assets effected by most Western states. In helping to consolidate clericalism, the crisis served the interests of ideology in the short run, but it has hurt it in the long term.

Fervid attachment to ideological ideals in the Iran-Iraq War has had negative as well as positive impact. The problems associated with this war are legion: high rates of inflation, rapid rise in the cost of living, high levels of unemployment, declining gross fixed domestic capital formation, idle plant capacity, low productivity in certain sectors, shortages of spare parts, scarcity of commodities and concomitant rationing (with the corruption associated with its administration), an active black market, brain drain and shortage of skilled personnel, excessive imports and negative balance of trade. True, not all these problems have been caused by the war, but those that have not are nevertheless seriously aggravated by it. Ironically for the regime, doctrinal rigidity may be pushing the Iranian state into the very pattern of rentier development so closely associated with the Pahlavi state. The rentier state is one whose economy depends heavily on revenue from a resource that is virtually independent of the factors of production for its production and sale. Oil revenues, in this particular case, are treated as pure economic rent, with almost no spillover effect into bona fide industrialization and/ or agricultural development. The revolutionary regime promised it would not follow the model of the shah's regime, but so far one would have to say that it is proceeding down the same road.

The authors of the essays dealing with Iran's foreign relations have implicitly shown that ideology is a major factor in political dynamics in Iran since 1979. They also infer that this ideology is "in trouble." The writers of the earlier chapters also suggest the importance of ideology. While they may differ on whether *velayat-e faqih* is radically new (Bayat) or in some sense in dialectical relationship with strands of classic Iranian culture (Hanaway), they are agreed on the urgency of this regime's moral vision. It remains to be seen whether *velayat-e faqih* will survive Khomeini, but it seems from this vantage point that some interpretation of Shi'ism will furnish elites with a specific ideology for some time to come.

Notes

1. Daniel Bell, *The End of Ideology* (Glencoe: Free Press, 1960).
2. Louis Fischer, *The Life of Lenin* (New York: Harper and Row, 1964), p. 207.

3. Edward A. Shils, "The Concept and Function of Ideology," *International Encyclopaedia of the Social Sciences*, 2d ed. (New York: Macmillan, 1968), vol. 7, pp. 66–76.

4. Khomeini's major problem in Islamic government is that he cannot find a specific textual reference to the Imam's *ex ante* appointment of clerics to be their replacements in the absence of the Hidden Imam. He does refer to the famous *maqbula* 'Omar b. Hanzala, which mentions the sixth Imam's appointment of judges (*hakem/hokkam*) in the event of litigation between individuals, but the context of the hadith shows that such judges have very narrow jurisdictions over technical matters. Khomeini interprets the Arabic word *hakem* in its broader sense as "ruler" and uses the Persian word *farmanrava* (sovereign ruler) as a translation for it.

5. To view doctrine as rigidly codified in some timeless way is to risk reification of the concept. It seems more appropriate to view it as evolving in dialectical relationship with social reality.

6. Peter Berger, *The Sacred Canopy: Elements of a Sociological Theory of Religion* (Garden City: Anchor Books, 1969), esp. 155 ff.

PART I

The Islamic Revolution in Iran

NIKKI R. KEDDIE

Islamic Revivalism Past and Present, with Emphasis on Iran

1. Modern Islamic Revivalism and Secularism: A Comparative Approach

Islamic revivalist movements in the past two centuries have largely been militantly political movements, usually directed against Western conquest, colonization, or interference in Muslim lands. The dramatic revivalist movements of the last few years, most notably in Iran, contain novel features, but they are not completely new phenomena. They contrast sharply with the rather pro-Western Muslim liberalism typified by Mohammad 'Abdoh and his mainly middle- or upper-class followers, the Muslim liberalism that was long the center of attention for Western writers on recent Islam. Islamic revivalism has more affinity to Muslim movements less concerned to liberalize Islam on a Western model than to save Muslim peoples from the physical and religio-cultural encroachments of the West.

While movements in eighteenth-century Arabia and India have certain affinities to later Islamic revivalism, I will here begin with the nineteenth century, when Western conquests in the Middle East began and when the industrial revolution and the resultant change in the character of world trade and production greatly increased the impact of the West on the Middle East. While the entry of Western goods in increased amounts and the consequent harm to Middle Eastern handicrafts brought some protests against the West, a true militant and military revivalism, largely in the name of defending Islam, came only in the face of actual Western military conquests and attempts to extend them. Interestingly, the early examples ("early" in terms of when major Western encroachments began) of military-political resistance were tied to "Sufi" religious orders with a large popular base. (The Western term "Sufi order" is misleading, as it conjures up a picture of other-worldly mystics.) Many tariqas—"orders" or "religious orders" minus the "Sufi" might be the best translation—were societies with a variety of social, economic,

3

political, and religious purposes in which mysticism might play little
or no part.

There is no space to detail tariqa-related resistance to Western encroachments, which included a defense of Islam and some revivalist
ideology, but three major examples of it may be mentioned: that of
'Abd al-Qader and his followers in Algeria against the French, that of
Shamyl in the Caucasus against the Russians, and that of the Sanusis
of Libya against the Italians. To some degree the Mahdist movement
of the Sudan in the 1880s and 1890s fits the pattern, as it appealed to
a tariqa, even though it was distinguished by a messianic ideology and
only partly directed against Europeans. According to Peter Holt, the
main socioeconomic change encouraging the Mahdist movement was
the end of the slave trade, with the economic difficulties this brought
in the Sudan, and this was a direct result of Western presence and
influence.[1]

All the above movements were, after decades of struggle, defeated,
and this is probably one reason they have not been given the attention
they merit in histories of the Middle East. They may be seen in a sense
as archaic, but they were not purely traditional; all managed to unite
unusually large groups of people in armed struggle over an unusually
long period of time. Their armed struggle and the relative success they
had with it (relative, for example, to recent urban guerrillas) shows their
hold on, and ideological ties to, the masses of ordinary people who
made up their followers—a hold and influence never matched by middle-
class Muslim liberals with ties to the West. There is a direct similarity,
and perhaps an indirect tie, between these leaders and the Algerian
and other revolutionaries of the post–World War II period who similarly
called upon the Islamic and anti-infidel feelings of ordinary people.

After the defeat of these armed movements, primacy seemed to pass
to Westernized Muslim liberals, but this is in part an illusion of Western
and Middle Eastern intellectuals, who tended not only to play down
what ordinary people were thinking and doing but also to stress one
side of the thought and action of those they regarded as liberals and
reformers. A prime example of this one-sidedness is seen in the treatment
of Sayyed Jamal ad-Din "al-Afghani" (who was born and raised in Iran).
Many writers stress his few words favoring constitutions and reforms,
but a careful analysis of all his writings and activities leads one to the
conclusion that his main concern was to strengthen the Muslim world
against Western encroachments by whatever means were most efficacious,
including military alliances and battles and an expedient use of the
literalist religious sentiment that he knew was still strongly felt by most
Muslims.[2] Jamal ad-Din was one representative of the so-called pan-
Islamic movement that threw some of the same terror into the hearts

of many Western leaders as does "Islamic resurgence" today. As with the early military resistance movements, there are parallels between pan-Islam and today's Islamic revival, but also important differences. Both movements are in part a reaction to new Western encroachments. Pan-Islam, while it was apparently first written about in logical detail by a liberal Young Ottoman, Namik Kemal, and while it drew on unclear claims of the Ottoman sultans to some kind of suzerainty over all Muslims (implied in a treaty with Russia in 1774, which gave Russia such rights over Orthodox subjects of the Ottoman Empire), became a widespread movement only with the growth of Western encroachments in the Middle East. Significantly, appeals to the Ottoman sultan for protection came step by step as reactions to Western encroachments on Muslim territory, first from Indian Muslims facing British conquest and then from Central Asian Muslims facing Russian conquest. The idea of Muslim unity, largely around Sultan 'Abd al-Hamid, who pushed the pan-Islamic idea even more than had his predecessor, spread in the Middle East with Russian conquests of Ottoman territory in their 1877–78 war, the French protectorate over Tunisia in 1881, and the British invasion of Egypt in 1882 (with British suppression of a resistance movement around Urabi that had some religious-messianic elements).[3]

Although some pan-Islamic theorists, such as Afghani and Namik Kemal, had certain reformist ideas, their concern for reform (especially Afghani's) was increasingly instrumental: reform, especially in the military and the government, was seen as a way of fending off Western encroachments. Hence it is not surprising that Afghani stressed hostility to British intrusion more than reform or that he accepted Sultan 'Abd al-Hamid's invitation to spend his last years in Istanbul, where his voice was largely muffled. As with today's Islamic revival, the pan-Islamists ranged from right to left on the political scale and were united mainly by their hostility to Western conquest and control. As a sidelight, it is interesting to note that British Foreign Office and other documents show that some pan-Islamists backed the Sudanese Mahdi, even though his claims would necessarily override the claims of their sultan. Also, the beginning of the Muslim year 1300, when the Mahdi was active, saw some of the same pan-Islamic and anti-Western fervor as was observed in the opening of the year 1400 with the attack on the mosque in Mecca and other militant movements.[4]

The last mass movement around the pan-Islamic ideal was the Khelafa movement in post–World War I India. This too was largely directed against the British, but it proved impossible to defend a caliph who was deposed by his own Turkish ruler, Ataturk.[5] Nevertheless, feelings of Muslim identity, particularly in the face of a West seen as dominant and hostile, remain strong in the Muslim world and are an important element in today's Islamic revival.

The first group with the organizational and ideological features associated with many contemporary movements of Islamic revival was the Egyptian Muslim Brotherhood, formed in 1928 and continuing, through many periods of illegality and repression, up to the present. Although at the time of its formation it seemed unique, many of its elements were harbingers of later Muslim movements: (1) The group was headed not by one of the leading ulama, but by a lay Muslim, and on the whole the leading ulama avoided it. (2) It had a populist appeal; not only could it call upon a large and broad base of support, but it appealed to the lower middle classes and often to the common people and was not oriented toward reconciling its ideas, except at a relatively elementary level, with unfamiliar modern Western theories. (3) It retained and defended much more of traditional Islamic law and practice than did reformers like Mohammad 'Abdoh, not attempting, for example, any radical change in male-female relationships or attitudes toward morality and the family. Its interpretations of Islam included some changes from what was "traditional," but there was no idea that the "traditional" should be scuttled in favor of a thinly disguised Westernism. (4) It had a social program designed to meet the needs of the poor and the petty bourgeoisie. The idea that Islam, with its high ideals, provided a better means of handling socioeconomic problems than either Western capitalism or Western socialism was increasingly embodied in Muslim Brotherhood writings and spread to other revivalist groups. (5) It did not shun the use of violence against individuals or groups if violence were seen as leading to important ends. (6) It saw Islamically oriented resistance as the best, perhaps the only, way to get rid of the British presence in Egypt and what Muslims largely saw as the similar Western Zionist presence in Palestine.

The Muslim Brotherhood, organized into secret cells, has had considerable influence in Egypt, although it is now considered too moderate by more radical and militant groups, such as the one responsible for Anwar Sadat's assassination. Since World War II there have been groups using the name of Muslim Brotherhood in Syria and other Muslim countries, but it is unclear how much they are directed by or even tied to the Egyptian one, which has itself undergone considerable transformation with the death or execution of many of its leaders and recurrent periods of effective illegality.[6]

In Iran, the first of the contemporary Islamic revival groups bore some resemblance in ideology to the Egyptian Muslim Brotherhood but was much smaller, less sophisticated, and less ideologically influential, its influence coming mostly from its assassinations. This was the Feda'iyyin-e Islam, founded near the end of World War II by the young and barely educated Navvab Safavi. Among its assassinations were those of the great intellectual and writer critical of Shi'ism, Ahmad Kasravi, and of the prime minister who tried to negotiate an oil agreement with the British, General 'Ali Razmara. This was followed by the Mosaddeq government (1951–53), in which mass feeling was so strong that Razmara's assassin was freed. The Feda'iyyin were for a time protected by a prominent ulama leader, Ayatollah Sayyed Abu 'l-Qasem Kashani.[7] After Mohammad Mosaddeq's overthrow with U.S. and British aid, the Feda'iyyin leaders were executed, and their small number meant that they did not go on to assume the role of Egypt's Muslim Brotherhood. It is even unclear what significance to give to the claims of the "hanging judge" Khalkhali and a few others that they are long-time members of the Feda'iyyin-e Islam.

In the forties and fifties, then, Egypt had a fairly sizable revivalist organization with roots going back to 1928, while Iran's revivalist group was small and weak and could influence events only because it assassinated leaders and tied into some of the aims of a secular nationalist movement. To some extent the latter was true of Egypt too; Gamal Abdel Nasser's Free Officers, with Sadat as their intermediary, were in contact with the Muslim Brotherhood before Nasser came to power, and both sides must have hoped for continued collaboration. Nasser's secularism and activities, however, made him the target of an assassination attempt plausibly blamed on the Muslim Brotherhood, which was outlawed as a result. The Iranian situation before Mosaddeq was parallel; the Feda'iyyin saw Prime Minister Razmara as a tool of the West, much as Nasser and the Brotherhood saw King Faruq, and the secular leader could temporarily accept aid from revivalist terrorists on the way to power. Once in power, however, Mosaddeq was as threatened by the Feda'iyyin as was Nasser by the Brotherhood, and both secular leaders moved against the revivalists who could no longer be counted as supporters. British power was opposed by all the above parties, but this was not enough to make them permanent allies.

Another broad similarity between the Egyptian and Iranian cases was the failure of Western-style nationalism and secularism under Nasser and Mosaddeq fully to meet the social and cultural needs of the two peoples. Although the patterns of the two countries since 1951 are not at all identical, some comparisons may be made. The rise of Mosaddeq in 1951 and of the Free Officers in 1952 (with Naguib as the first titular head, soon replaced by Nasser) both represented moves for national independence and against foreign, especially British, control. This was indicated in Mosaddeq's immediate nationalization of the British-owned

oil industry and Nasser's 1956 nationalization of the Suez Canal, both
of which were greeted in the Western press and by Western governments
with a horror that can scarcely be imagined today. Most significant in
the present context is the fact that both the Mosaddeq movement and
the Free Officers' movement were secularist and highly popular. It seems
clear that there is no age-old ingrained religiosity among either Iranians
or Egyptians that means that only a leader who speaks in Islamic religious
terms can be popular. Mosaddeq was widely and wildly popular, with
his popularity falling off somewhat only when it became clear that he
had no solution to the Western-imposed loss of oil income that began
to bring a decline in Iranian living standards. Nasser was similarly
popular, even when he took more radical socialist measures than Mosaddeq dreamed of, thus alienating an upper stratum of his supporters.
His loss of popularity came mainly over foreign policy issues—the great
economic and human drain caused by the Yemeni War and the loss to
Israel in 1967. Secularism as such did not end with Mosaddeq's fall; if
anything, the newly dictatorial Mohammad Reza Shah was more aggressively secular than Mosaddeq. Under him secularism did become
unpopular, not only because it was more aggressively pursued than
before but because it was associated with Western control or influence.[8]

The growing association of secularism with Western control or influence was one important factor in the new wave of Islamic revivalism
that began in Iran, Egypt, and other Muslim countries in the 1960s.
The perception of Western advance was based on a combination of
factors, some of which were exaggerated in the popular view but all
of which had a considerable basis in reality.

One of the oldest and strongest components in the perception of
Western encroachment in the Middle East was the formation and continued expansion of the state of Israel, which is almost universally
viewed in the Muslim world as an illegitimate Western implantation or
colony with expansionist designs. For a time arguments against Israel,
especially by the educated, tended to be secularist, especially since the
Palestinians included a large Christian minority, some of whom headed
important resistance groups. Part of the standard argument against Israel
was that it was a theocratic state basing full citizenship on religion,
while the Palestinians wished to form a state in which all religious
groups would be equal. With the victory of the "theocratic" Israelis
against the secularist Nasser in 1967, however, growing numbers of
Muslims and Arabs began to think that perhaps the very religious
commitment of the Israelis, which they probably exaggerated, was a
major secret of their strength and that increased commitment to Islam
would bring increased solidarity and militance. Also, the Israeli conquest
of the West Bank and especially the old city of Jerusalem, with the

events at al-Aqsa mosque soon afterwards, revived a Muslim identification around the Israel and Palestine issues in terms that were more specifically Islamic than before. Khomeini and other activist religious leaders in Iran stressed the issue as much as did Arabs.

Another aspect of Western encroachment and Westernization felt in Iran, Egypt, and other Muslim countries was the association of conservative, Westernizing, secularizing leaders, notably Mohammad Reza Shah and Sadat, with increasingly unpopular economic, political, and cultural measures. There was no massive criticism of the secularism of Mosaddeq and Nasser because their measures were mostly, and with reason, popular. Both pursued internally oriented economic policies, building up new industries (and expanding old ones) with a very large measure of internal control. They did not allow their countries' economies to be dominated by the consumerist values, oriented toward the wealthy, that became notable when their successors adopted policies pleasing to the West and to large Western corporations. Naturally there were many, particularly among the wealthier classes, who resented the belt-tightening and government controls that Nasser and Mosaddeq imposed in order to build up a more balanced and less class-divided economy less dependent on the West, but although many were critical of this or that approach, there were few who rejected the whole. Even though some religious leaders (like some secular leaders) broke with Mosaddeq, there was nothing like the later religious opposition to the shah, and the same may be said of Nasser vis-à-vis Sadat. In other words, secularist leadership alone was not enough to elicit a significant Islamic revival; it came only with a leadership associated with Western encroachments and with material dissatisfactions on the part of rural migrants, students, and the traditional petty bourgeoisie.

Although Mohammad Reza Shah and Sadat appeared to be, and in many ways were, very different figures, in relation to policies that encouraged religious revival they showed significant similarities. Both (Mohammad Reza for a longer period) were seen as betrayers of the Muslim cause regarding Israel—the shah by selling oil to Israel and using Israeli advisers in many spheres, including SAVAK, and Sadat by making a separate peace and abandoning his Asian Arab neighbors, who were surely too weak to fight Israel alone. Both were seen as essentially allies, if not lackeys, of the United States and its Western allies rather than followers of the nonaligned policy that had characterized Mosaddeq and Nasser and that had mass appeal.

In the economic sphere, while Nasser after 1967 had begun to move in the direction of free enterprise, the changes brought by Sadat's "open-door policy" were more dramatic and harmful for most Egyptians. Instead of maintaining the controls vital to a country with so small a land and resource base and so large and growing a population, Sadat was persuaded by U.S. and other advisers that removing these controls would bring greatly increased foreign investment and hence prosperity. The end of controls flooded the Egyptian market with foreign consumer goods, undermined local industries, encouraged agricultural mechanization in an overpopulated countryside, brought a flood of people to overcrowded cities, created inflation, and increased corruption and the gap between rich and poor. Even though Iran had greater wealth, especially after 1973, the results of its encouragement of a Western-oriented economy favoring the rich were quite similar; the basic needs of ordinary people lost out to imported or locally assembled hard goods for the prosperous; agricultural mechanization and population growth made the poor stream to the cities, and growing corruption, the increased income-distribution gap, and resentment against corrupt rulers, businessmen, and foreigners made migrants, students, and the bazaar classes ready to follow a new oppositional ideology.

Once secularism, in Egypt, Iran, and elsewhere, came to be firmly associated with leaders seen as "selling" their countries to the West and Israel, and in situations in which secular oppositionists could scarcely function, it is not surprising that the ideas of roots and authenticity and an idealized version of the past came to be associated with Islam. This was facilitated by the fact that actual Islamic governments lay in the dim past, while nationalism, parliamentarianism, socialism, modern autocracy, and other supposed panaceas, mostly of Western origin, had all been tried (or were believed to have been tried) in the Middle East and found wanting. Both the shah in the mid-fifties and Sadat after Nasser's death placated the religious activists, who were seen as useful against leftist or democratic opponents, but instead of winning them over increased their visibility and inviolability. Although Egypt's ulama leadership is generally subservient to its rulers and very different from Iran's, popular sentiments in the two countries have many similarities, and a populist, fundamentalist national religious leadership is not to be ruled out in Egypt's future.[9]

2. Islamic Revivalism in Power in Iran

Outside of Iran, no government exists that was brought to power by a populist Islamic movement and is carrying out many of the goals of that movement. The Saudi Arabian state has its roots in an Islamic revivalist movement that goes back to the eighteenth century, but today the "Islamic" measures enforced by the Saudi state—notably women's segregation and "Quranic" rules against drinking, gambling, charging interest, and the like—are widely regarded as, in part, window-dressing, followed by the elite in public but not in private. The true revivalists, like those who took over the mosque in Mecca, are hostile to the Saudi government.

Zia' al-Haqq's military rule in Pakistan is, somewhat similarly, widely regarded as having adopted some "Quranic" rules and punishments in order to gain strength and popularity. Some of his measures have instead led to discord. An attempt to have the government collect the religious *zakat* tax was angrily and successfully protested by the Shi'is, whose ulama, there as in Iran, have never given up their right to collect religious taxes. Moves against coeducation and other women's rights have also aroused some protests. Zia's 1981 "provisional constitutional order," while giving lip-service to Islam, puts all final decisions in his hands and not in those of any Islamic body.

Qadhdhafi of Libya, who early in his rule adopted some Islamic measures and rhetoric, has increasingly moved toward secularism in both his writings and his actions, and it is an anachronism to regard his reign as significantly tied to Islamic revivalism.[10] Some of the small Arab Gulf states have codified Islamic measures but not primarily as a result of populist Islamic movements.

To date the true revivalists have taken power only in Iran. This locus is not surprising and arises partly from the continued power, independence, and periodic struggles against the government, unmatched in any other country, of part of the Iranian Shi'i ulama. Among the factors that account for this are the relative decentralization of pre-Pahlavi Iran, the independent income of the ulama and their control of religious taxes, the location of the leading Shi'i ulama outside Iran from the eighteenth until well into the twentieth century, and the close ties of the ulama to the bazaar classes. The militant secularism of the increasingly unpopular Pahlavi shahs and their successful suppression of liberal or leftist secular opponents left the oppositional ulama the only group that could organize and influence large numbers of opponents to the government with relative impunity. From the 1960s on, revivalist opposition grew in theory and practice, and various studies have shown how, aided by the charismatic Ayatollah Khomeini, it came to lead the mixed revolutionary movement of 1978–79.[11]

Less well known or analyzed are trends since the victory of that revolution. In a general way, the Iranian revolution fits the pattern set forth in Crane Brinton's *Anatomy of Revolution*, in which an initial movement toward ever greater radicalism and purism culminating in a regime of "terror and virtue" is followed by a "Thermidor," which now appears to be under way in Iran. The Iranian revolution differs from the French and some others in that what may be called its "Thermidor" has come not with the overthrow of those who may be called radicals in government, but with the giving of greater weight to right-wingers and to those who once favored the radicals but now act conservatively. The radicals are, as of January 1984, still in government, and some are still fighting for greater influence. In social terms the recent development has been away from workers and peasants and toward the middle, landed, and professional classes—including bazaaris, landlords and wealthy peasants, and professionals and technocrats, as well as those in these classes and among students outside Iran whom the government would like to attract back to Iran. Revolutionary utopianism has, at least for now, partly given way to "bourgeois" practicality, including a stress on oil income, foreign trade, and technology, though continued war, jailings, executions, and anti-American rhetoric have kept most Americans from noticing the change.

Both Iranian revolutionaries and some foreign analysts have divided the revolution in power into three phases, and the Thermidor beginning sometime in 1982 may be added as a fourth.

The first phase began with the seizure of power by guerrilla forces in the name of the revolution in February 1979 and ended with the taking of the American hostages in November 1979. At first there was a true united-front government, including not only nonulama supporters of Khomeini, notably Prime Minister Mahdi Bazargan and the younger Abu 'l-Hasan Bani-Sadr, Sadeq Qotbzada, and Ibrahim Yazdi, but also, for a time, more conservative, secularist members of the National Front such as Karim Sanjabi. For a time there was considerable freedom of the press and association, but by the summer of 1979 numerous newspapers and journals had been suppressed, and the clerically backed thugs called the Hezbollahis were breaking up demonstrations by leftist and left-center groups, notably the Mojahedin-e Khalq, the Feda'iyyin-e Khalq, and the National Democratic Front led by Hedayatollah Matin-Daftari, a grandson of Mosaddeq.

With the taking of the U.S. embassy and hostages, the movement toward control by radical clerics received a big impetus that the growing radical clerical leadership used for its own ends; this inaugurated the second phase of the revolution. Bazargan and his foreign minister Yazdi resigned when they were unable to resolve the crisis, and their power passed to radical clerics. In the light of later trends, the January 1980 election of Bani-Sadr as president appears in part as an anomaly that occurred largely because the Islamic Republican Party candidate was forbidden to run because of a technicality. Iraq's attack on Iran later in 1980 further radicalized the situation and made opponents of the regime, such as the Kurds, who had been fighting for autonomy since negotiations broke down in 1979, look like traitors. Bani-Sadr's position as commander-in-chief did not increase his long-term power and was taken from him in 1981.

The third phase began in the spring and early summer of 1981, when participants in a Bani-Sadr rally, attacked by the Hezbollahis, fought back, and Bani-Sadr was stripped of his presidency and went into hiding. He escaped abroad with Mas'ud Rajavi, leader of the Islamic leftist Mojahedin-e Khalq, which declared its militant opposition to the regime. A large number of assassinations of high- and middle-level governmental figures, mostly by the Mojahedin, failed to weaken the government but did give it both a reason and an excuse to crack down on all opposition, which was tainted with abetting the Iraqi enemy. Executions, torture, and jailings occurred on a massive scale.

During these three phases the government tried to meet some of the needs of the poor, despite the economic problems created by revolution and war, and the volunteer Construction Crusade carried out important public works while organizations like the Foundation for the Oppressed aided the urban poor. New land distribution measures were proposed from 1980 on but never implemented, although some confiscations effected by peasants were not reversed.

The fourth phase began with conservative measures early in 1982, and by the end of that year, this tendency was clear, even though there were few major personnel changes after those necessitated by the assassinations. One aspect of this phase has been the veto by the Council of Guardians as un-Islamic of economic measures that were deemed to interfere with private property (in contrast to the numerous national-izations that had taken place earlier). The two main measures so vetoed in 1982 were a land reform bill, which would have divided still-existing large holdings among poor peasants, and one nationalizing most foreign trade. Iranian eyewitness reports indicate that pressure from landowners and bazaar elements whose economic interests would be hurt by these measures help account for these vetoes; both laws had been passed by the Majlis, which still represents more broad-based popular opinion.

In late 1982 Khomeini issued a decree that, among other things, protected people's homes, jobs, and telephones against scrutiny or invasion by officials, and this was followed by the creation of investigative bodies that traveled throughout Iran and the forced resignation of some officials charged with crimes against people. Khomeini spoke of the revolutionary phase's being over and the need for stabilization. Middle-class and upper-class pressures were at work here too, as was the growing economic pragmatism also seen in Iran's striving for high oil production and prices and numerous trade and industrial agreements with a variety of countries that could not meet Iran's ideological standards. The establishment of some new legal norms, as long as the persons involved were not Baha'is, women, or associated with organizations considered hostile, was aimed in large part at the middle classes and at halting the continued emigration of trained persons and attracting back such persons who had gone abroad. The conservatism has often not, however, been directed toward legal norms. The increasing arms sales by the USSR to Iraq after Iran refused to negotiate with the latter were probably the main reason for the arrest early in 1983 of the leadership of the Tuda party and the effective banning of that party despite its support of the government. Jailings and/or executions of people for their associations—whether Mojahedin, Tuda, or Baha'i—continue and often involve the flouting of legal norms.

The 1982 veto of the land reform bill was both an element and a directional signal in the treatment of peasants. The increasing references to the sanctity of private property in Islam have found their most extreme expression to date in a labor act proposed in 1983, which would do away with both the gains made before the revolution and those added in some areas since then. Islam is said in this bill to sanction what amounts to the view enforced in parts of the West at the beginning of the nineteenth century, namely, no interference of any sort with private contracts between owner and worker. Group gains, including unions, insurance, and a minimum wage, would be outlawed, as would existing limits on child labor. In a period of mass unemployment like the present, workers would surely bid each other downward. Whether or not the measure passes in its current form, it is a good indication of the way some of those now leading the government look at socio-economic issues.[12] The dismissal in the summer of 1983 of the Minister of Labor who sponsored the bill put the bill in limbo, but its ideas were not repudiated by its supporters.

As I have said, it is a special feature of the Iranian Thermidor that it is being carried out largely by the same persons who were identified with the radical Phase 3 and, in some cases, with even earlier phases. It is common both in the Muslim world and elsewhere for someone who begins with a radical and populist appeal to adjust to the old ruling classes and conservative ways once in power, but here there has been, in addition, a postrevolutionary phase of increasing radicalism reminiscent of revolutions like the French, in which personnel did change. It appears that revolutions do have a momentum and force that pushes them, once in power, toward fulfillment of some of their promises to the masses and suppression of less revolutionary views. In the English, French, and Russian revolutions, foreign war was another force leading to greater radicalism and to both voluntary and forced unification of the nation behind the embattled revolution, and this has also happened in Iran. These parallels with non-Islamic movements, as well as the ease with which many of Iran's clerical leaders can change their interpretations of Islam from revolutionary-populist to conservative-bourgeois, indicate that Islamic ideology is malleable according to circumstances. Both radical and conservative camps still exist among the ulama, with Khomeini bowing to trends more than is admitted, and future trends cannot be divined by any study of Shi'ism, which is constantly in flux.

Since the 1960s, Islamic revival in Iran, while appealing to some of the same mass sentiments, has represented a wide variety of trends in practice. Even if one starts an analysis only in 1978, one finds a variety of ideas bound together at first more by a common enemy—the shah and his foreign supporters—than by a really common interpretation of Islam. Interpretations ranged from the de facto socialism of the Mojahedin-e Khalq through the more ambiguous radicalism associated with the name of 'Ali Shari'ati (d. 1977), the reformism of Mortaza Motahhari, and the rather conservative bazaar-oriented constitutionalism of Kazem Shari'atmadari, to the populist fundamentalism of Khomeini. Younger nonclerical followers of Khomeini such as Bani-Sadr, Qotbzada, and Yazdi seem to have believed that their influence on Khomeini's pronouncements in France, which Khomeini accepted out of pragmatism, would extend to a real moderating influence after the revolution, but it did not. Bani-Sadr has subsequently claimed to have been betrayed by Khomeini, but he seems rather to have believed in that part of the prerevolutionary Khomeini that pleased him.[13]

After the revolution there continued to be ideological differences, not only including all the above groups, but centering more and more on continuing differences between radical and conservative ruling clergy, among whom there were often shifting alliances and subfactions. As noted above, policies have changed significantly from one phase of the revolution to the next, and for each phase and policy an Islamic justification has been found. The few constants that might be noted have been in enforcing "Islamic" laws and some "Islamic" punishments (in quotation marks because there is no complete agreement, even among Shi'is, about what laws and punishments are Islamic). These are mostly, as elsewhere, in the sphere of what we would call morality and in the segregation of women and a return to many Quranic or early Islamic laws regarding marriage and the family. Bad treatment of the Baha'is has also been present in all phases. Essentially, then, a considerable number of Baha'is, active oppositionists, and women have borne a burden in all phases of the revolutionary movement from at least Phase 2 on.[14]

Another constant of the Islamic Revolution in power, which ties it to the Islamic revivalist movements discussed in the first part of this article, is its anti-imperialist appeal. The "Great Satan," the United States, remains the great symbolic enemy, responsible for most of Iran's problems, though it is increasingly joined by the USSR. Iraq is seen as a surrogate of one or both.[15] France gets its share of lumps for arming Iraq and hosting the major political leaders in exile. Also, the revolution suggests that anti-Israeli feeling in Iran is stronger than most outsiders realized. I witnessed the first of the annual "Jerusalem Days" on the fourth Friday of Ramadan, and the crowds in and around Tehran University were estimated at two million. Placards featuring Khomeini with Yaser Arafat have presumably been replaced since Arafat has come to be seen as a sellout, but militant sentiment for the recapture of Jerusalem and the West Bank does not seem to have diminished.

For all the changes within Islam in each country and within Islamic revivalist and revolutionary movements, anti-imperialism,[16] now focused on the United States and Israel, appears to be a constant feature from the beginnings of modern Islamic revivalism until today. If Islamic leaders in power do no more to meet the problems of their people than did the secularists, one may expect a decline in revivalism, at least where revivalists have tasted power. But until local economies and cultures are transformed to the point of providing for the basic needs of the majority and lessening the hegemony of outside powers, the revivalist phenomenon may always be revived.

Notes

1. P. M. Holt, *The Mahdist State in the Sudan, 1881–1898* (Oxford: Oxford University Press, 1958), and John Voll, "Mahdis, Walis, and the New Men in the Sudan," in *Scholars, Saints, and Sufis*, ed. Nikki R. Keddie (Berkeley and Los Angeles: University of California Press, 1972). See also E. E. Evans-Pritchard, *The Sanusi of Cyrenaica* (London: Oxford University Press, 1949), and Marcel Emerit, *L'Algerie à l'époque d'Abd-el-Kader* (Paris, 1951).

2. See the translations and analyses of his words and writings in Nikki R. Keddie, *An Islamic Response to Imperialism*, augmented paper and library ed. (Berkeley and Los Angeles: University of California Press, 1983), and *Sayyid Jamal ad-Din "al-Afghani": A Political Biography* (Berkeley and Los Angeles: University of California Press, 1972). Most of his important writings have appeared in several editions, including the Persian *Maqalat-e Jamaliyya* and the reprinted lead articles of the Arabic *al-'Orvat al-vothqa*.

3. See especially Albert Hourani, *Arabic Thought in the Liberal Age, 1798–1939* (London: Oxford University Press, 1962), pp. 103–7, and Niyazi Berkes, *The Development of Secularism in Turkey* (Montreal: McGill University Press, 1964), pp. 253–56.

4. Documents about Islamic response to the Mahdi and the year 1300 may be found in the British Foreign Office.

5. An important recent scholarly work on the subject is Gail Minault, *The Khilafat Movement: Religious Symbolism and Political Mobilization in India* (New

York: Columbia University Press, 1982). See also W. C. Smith, *Modern Islam in India* (London: Victor Gollancz, 1946).

6. On the Muslim Brotherhood, see especially Christina P. Harris, *Nationalism and Revolution in Egypt: The Role of the Muslim Brotherhood* (The Hague: Mouton, 1964), and, for the recent period, Nazih N. M. Ayubi, "The Political Revival of Islam: The Case of Egypt," *International Journal of Middle East Studies* 12 (1980):481–99. See also Richard P. Mitchell, *The Society of the Muslim Brothers* (London: Oxford University Press, 1969).

7. See Yann Richard, "Ayatollah Kashani: Precursor of the Islamic Republic?" in *Religion and Politics in Iran: Shi'ism from Quietism to Revolution*, ed. Nikki R. Keddie (New Haven: Yale University Press, 1983); Nikki R. Keddie and A. H. Zarrinkub, "Fida'iyyan-i Islam," in *Encyclopedia of Islam*, 2d ed.; and the forthcoming article on the Feda'iyyin by Farhad Kazemi. I interviewed Ayatollah Kashani in 1960 and take a somewhat more skeptical view of him than does Richard. See also Amir H. Ferdows, "Khomaini and Fadayan's Society and Politics," *International Journal of Middle East Studies* 15 (1983):241–57.

8. New analyses of Mosaddeq should soon be available, as the British are releasing documents after the legal thirty-year interval. The United States, which should have opened its documents on the period before now, has held them back and, reportedly, has withheld so many documents that even when the others are released there will be serious omissions. Pending studies based partly on such documents, see the analyses in Richard Cottam, *Nationalism in Iran*, new ed. (Pittsburgh: University of Pittsburgh Press, 1979); Ervand Abrahamian, *Iran between Two Revolutions* (Princeton: Princeton University Press, 1982); and Nikki R. Keddie, *Roots of Revolution: An Interpretive History of Modern Iran* (New Haven: Yale University Press, 1981). On Egypt, see John Waterbury, *The Egypt of Nasser and Sadat* (Princeton: Princeton University Press, 1983), and his sources, and M. H. Kerr and E. Yassin, eds., *Rich and Poor States in the Middle East* (Boulder: Westview Press, 1982).

9. Of the myriad works dealing with Islamic revival since the 1960s, see especially Edward Mortimer, *Faith and Power: The Politics of Islam* (New York: Vintage Books, 1982); Nikki R. Keddie, ed., *Religion and Politics in Iran*, especially the articles by S. Akhavi, W. Floor, A Tabari, W. Beeman, and G. Rose and the introduction; Shahrough Akhavi, *Religion and Politics in Contemporary Iran* (Albany: State University of New York Press, 1980); James P. Piscatori, ed., *Islam in the Political Process* (Cambridge: Cambridge University Press, 1983), especially Fouad Ajami on Egypt: and Olivier Carré, ed., *L'Islam et l'état dans le monde d'aujourd'hui* (Paris: Presses Universitaires de France, 1982). See also Ayubi, "The Political Revival of Islam," and his "The Politics of Militant Islamic Movements in the Middle East," *Journal of International Affairs*, Fall/Winter 1982–83, pp. 271–83; Saad Eddin Ibrahim, "Anatomy of Egypt's Militant Islamic Groups: Methodological Note and Preliminary Findings," *International Journal of Middle East Studies* 12 (1980):423–53; and N. R. Keddie, "Islamic Revival as Third Worldism," in *Le cuisinier et le philosophe: Hommage à Maxime Rodinson*, ed. J.-P. Digard (Paris: Maisonneuve et Larose, 1982). See also Ibrahim Abu-Lughod, ed., *The Islamic Alternative* (Arab Studies Quarterly 4 [Spring 1982]).

10. See the sections on Pakistan and Qadhdhafi in Mortimer, *Faith and Power,* Piscatori, *Islam in the Political Process,* and Carré, *L'Islam et l'état.* See also the chapters by Ann E. Mayer and Mumtaz Ahmad in *Islam in the Contemporary World,* ed. C. K. Pullapilly (Notre Dame: Cross Roads Books, 1980).

11. See the relevant parts of Abrahamian, *Iran;* Akhavi, *Religion and Politics;* Keddie, *Roots of Revolution;* Fred Halliday, *Iran: Dictatorship and Development* (New York: Penguin, 1979); Robert Graham, *Iran: The Illusion of Power* (London: Croom Helm, 1979); Eric Hooglund, *Land and Revolution in Iran: 1960–1980* (Austin: University of Texas Press, 1982); and F. Kazemi, ed., *Iranian Revolution in Perspective* (Iranian Studies 13 [1980]). See also various writings by Shaul Bakhash, mainly in the *New York Review of Books,* and his forthcoming book on Khomeini's Iran, and the writings of R. K. Ramazani, Sepehr Zabih, and Said Arjomand. In 1978 Khomeini's somewhat liberal-sounding pronouncements were far better known in Iran and among Iranian oppositionists abroad than was his 1971 *Hokumat-e Eslami* and other strongly fundamentalist writings, which I was able to read in a Western library as early as 1973. For a revealing view from inside the old regime, see Daryush Homayun, *Diruz va Farda* (n.p. [U.S.], 1981).

12. Of the numerous sources discussing the course of the Iranian revolution, the most consistently useful may be the English and especially the Persian sections of the *Iran Times,* the broadcast translations in the Foreign Broadcast Information Service Reports, published by the U.S. Department of Commerce, and the rather similar British SWB reports. The Persian newspaper *Iranshahr* also has much useful information, including an article covering the restrictive labor bill published on February 18, 1983; on this law see also *Payam-e Azadi,* 15 Azar, 1341 (1983). On recent trends in the revolution I have read numerous articles in various languages and am also indebted to a May 1983 lecture by Ahmad Ashraf at the University of California, Los Angeles, and to an unpublished paper by Gary Sick. See also Elaine Sciolino, "Iran's Durable Revolution," *Foreign Affairs,* Spring 1983, pp. 893–920; Nikki R. Keddie and Eric Hooglund, eds., *The Iranian Revolution and the Islamic Republic* (Washington, D.C.: Middle East Institute and Woodrow Wilson Center, 1982); and Nikki R. Keddie, "Iranian Revolutions in Comparative Perspective," *AHR,* June, 1983. Also useful is U.S. House of Representatives, Committee on Foreign Affairs, *The Iran Hostage Crisis: A Chronology of Daily Developments* (Library of Congress, Congressional Research Service, or U.S. Government Printing Office, 1981), and the many volumes with different titles published reproducing U.S. documents by the "Muslim Students Following the Line of the Imam" in Tehran.

13. I saw this in my own conversations with Bani-Sadr in France in 1973 and 1981, and it also appears in other interviews he has given. His own utopian view of what an Islamic society means comes out in his *Eqtesad-e Tauhidi* (n.p. [Tehran?], n.d.).

14. See Iran Committee for Democratic Action and Human Rights, *Human Rights in the Islamic Republic of Iran* (Chicago, 1982); Eliz Sanasarian, *The Women's Rights Movement in Iran* (New York: Praeger, 1982); Lois Beck and Nikki Keddie, eds., *Women in the Muslim World* (Cambridge: Harvard University Press, 1978);

Adele K. Ferdows, "Women and the Islamic Revolution," *International Journal of Middle East Studies* 15 (1983):283–98; Farah Azari, ed., *Women of Iran* (London: Ithaca Press, 1983); and Azar Tabari and Nahid Yeganeh, eds., *In the Shadow of Islam* (London: Zed Press, 1982).

15. See S. Tahir-Kheli and S. Ayubi, eds., *The Iran-Iraq War* (New York: Praeger, 1983); Ali E. Hillal Dessouki, *The Iraq-Iran War* (Princeton: Princeton University Center of International Studies, 1981); and Tareq Y. Ismael, *Iraq and Iran: Roots of Conflict* (Syracuse: Syracuse University Press, 1982).

16. Some readers of this paper object to the use of "anti-imperialism" regarding rightists like Khomeini, but the only alternatives they suggest—"anti-foreign" or "anti-Western"—appear to me less accurate.

MANGOL BAYAT

Shi'a Islam as a Functioning Ideology in Iran: The Cult of the Hidden Imam

Unlike Sunnism, Shi'ism in its formative period allowed the elaboration of a concept of ideal leadership that, though identified with the abstract idea of the Hidden Imam (the idea that the twelfth successor of Mohammad had not died, but disappeared), was capable of providing a doctrinal rationale for sociopolitical protest against the established order. The doctrine of the Imamate, which theoretically denies legitimacy to any form of government, was rarely used to overthrow it. To quote a recent study, "a doctrine of potential resistance is not a doctrine of revolution."[1] The belief in the Imam as the repository of divine knowledge, the infallible teacher whose primary task is to perfect men's understanding of the prophetic revelation, did, however, enable Imami Shi'ism to develop a separate system of thought. Shi'i speculative thinkers, philosophers and mystics alike, carried on, in the name of the Hidden Imam, the task of spiritual and intellectual renewal. Though they accepted Mohammad's prophecy as the last and most complete of all revelations and the twelve imams' teachings as the true guide to the prophetic message, they were reluctant to accept the absence of direct leadership in times of *ghaiba* (occultation of the Imam). They insisted on the need for an uninterrupted chain of human mediators acting as spiritual representatives of the Hidden Imam. The concepts of the Philosopher-king, the Pole, the Perfect Man, the Perfect Shi'a, and the Fourth Pillar[2] are all variants of a single human ideal viewed by the esotericists and speculative thinkers as the "true leader." Though they generally conceded to the *foqaha'* (specialists in jurisprudence) the right to teach and apply the shari'a (Islamic law), a task they believed demanded no special spiritual or intellectual talent, they reserved for themselves the right to "renew" the dogma. Their scriptural interpretations of Shi'a works allowed them to offer their Muslim intellectual contemporaries a legitimate

21

but more progressive, more challenging and innovative view of knowledge as an alternative to the official teachings of the conservative theologians.

The foqaha', on the other hand, viewed the Imam as the sole authoritative source of knowledge and maintained that the renewed understanding of the revelation had to be postponed until the return of the Hidden Imam. As guardians of the law that regulates the everyday life of the believer in this world and prepares him for the next, they resisted and condemned the development of an individual leadership that laid claim to absolute authority in the name of the Imam. Nevertheless, despite the traditional stand of the jurists, occasional deviations from the norm may be observed. For instance, the concept of the *marja'-e taqlid-e motlaq* as the supreme authority in religious affairs, which gained ascendancy in the nineteenth century, demonstrates the jurists' own temptation to recognize the need for individual leadership. That this concept did not find firm roots in Imami Shi'ism is evidence of the sect's strong juridical preference for a collective leadership that allows a degree of *ekhtelaf*, divergence of opinion in legal matters not directly concerned with the basic principles of religion or with fundamental aspects of the dogma.

At the turn of the century, socioeconomic forces and new ideas shifted the emphasis in religious disputes from doctrinal considerations to politics. The lay modernists found "converts" to their political cause within the ranks of the dissident ulama and through them gained the valuable support of some high-ranking members of the religious establishment. A new conception of the law then split the opinion of the religious community. The state and the religious establishment had periodically clashed over their respective rights to administer the law. While the ulama had a monopoly over matters pertaining to personal and commercial law, the state enjoyed the right to administer public law, or *'orf*. The distinction between 'orf and shari'a and their application to particular cases was not always clear. Throughout the second half of the nineteenth century, government officials often clashed with the ulama, who accused the state of encroaching upon their legal domain and enlarging its jurisdiction at their expense. To a number of high-ranking ulama, including Ayatollah Fazlollah Nuri, who had initially supported the movement, the promulgation of the Constitution of 1906 and the subsequent establishment of the Majlis as a consultative assembly for legislation offered a unique means to institutionalize and control the 'orf system. The idea of collective leadership taking over from a despotic monarch the power to enact laws pertaining to the public life of the believers thus gained official recognition. It also constituted yet another Shi'i attempt at accommodating the state, a more up-to-date modus vivendi. In the words of the revolutionary preacher Jamal ad-Din, the Majlis served as *vali al-amr* (Holder of Supreme Authority) in the absence of the Imam.[3]

The first decade of the twentieth century marked the end of theological speculative ferment. It was also the beginning of a political era in which the crucial issues were no longer those of doctrine or of man's relation to the ultimate conditions of his existence. The dispute that came to divide the ranks of the religious establishment was over aspects of the new law. Both the opponents and the proponents of the new constitution favored the continued existence of the state, with its executive power delegated to a cabinet of ministers directly responsible to the Majlis. Nuri and fellow opponents of the constitution came to champion the cause of the reactionary Mohammad 'Ali Shah Qajar mainly as a result of their objection to the inclusion of certain articles. These articles, guaranteeing sovereignty of the people, freedom of opinion, equality of all citizens, including the religious minorities, before the law, and compulsory education for all men and women, were declared contrary to Islamic principles and directives. In fact, Nuri accused the Majlis of seeking to establish the "heretical" Babism and eradicate Islam in Iran. Yet members of the religious establishment occupied one-fourth of the seats of the Majlis that had drafted and unanimously adopted the new constitution. Moreover, a leading mojtahed of the time, Mohammad Hosain Na'ini, wrote in favor of the constitutional government. His often-quoted work[4] is nowadays hailed as an authentic Shi'i attempt at defining the form of government that would best fit the conditions of ghaiba. While Nuri's view was obviously influenced by his concern with the immediate threat of the Babi heresy (the ulama's main enemy at the time), Na'ini was undoubtedly inspired by Western concepts of constitutional rights.[5] The concerns of both men reflected the social tensions and clashing rhetorics of their time.

In the aftermath of the Constitutional Revolution, the poet, the lay man of letters, came to displace the mojtahed in influencing public opinion. The traditional centers of Islamic culture rapidly lost influence and prestige among progressive-minded thinkers. Change in intellectual outlook, traditionally initiated by speculative theologians and philosophers from within the ranks of the ulama, was undertaken by groups outside the religious establishment. However, the system of religious beliefs enforced by the ayatollahs was not openly rejected. Secularization, or the institutional change inaugurated by the first Majlis, was not accompanied by change in doctrine. Nor was secularism in its Western form adopted officially. The constitution specifically declared Twelver Shi'a Islam the state religion and granted a council of five mojtaheds the right to supervise Majlis legislation. Moreover, religious studies were made compulsory in public schools. The official anticlerical and mod-

ernizing policies of subsequent governments did not enforce the "shrink-
age in the character and extent of beliefs"[6] that Daniel Bell sees as
defining profanation. Similarly, twentieth-century intellectuals, though
freed from traditional clerical restraints, did not explore the alternatives
to religious answers as did their Western counterparts. In response to
their own disenchantment with traditional culture, they sought the means
for self-realization in nationalist politics, in modern scientific disciplines
imported from the West, and in new literary genres, leaving crucial
existential issues untouched. Metaphysics and philosophy in general
were neglected and thus remained, almost by default, the domain of
the turbaned ulama.

Nevertheless, the cult of the Hidden Imam remained intact at the
popular level throughout the 1960s and 1970s, despite the penetration
of modernism into rural areas through the literacy corps and enforced
military service. 'Ashura, the commemoration of the Third Imam's
martyrdom, was celebrated annually even in middle-class households.
Among the so-called Westernized intellectuals and artists, religious
symbols and rites were providing traditional roots for new modes of
literary self-expression and artistic creativity. *Ta'ziya*s (dramatizations of
Imam Hosain's martyrdom) were staged as Brechtian theater, as "hap-
penings." *Rauzakhani*s (religious recitals) were depicted as folktales just
as important as the epics of pre-Islamic heroes. Avant-garde movie
directors defended traditional customs and beliefs. The intellectuals'
defense of tradition and attacks on those who abused and took advantage
of the simple faith of the people offer a striking contrast to the literature
of revolt of the mid-nineteenth and early twentieth centuries, in which
popular religious rituals were ridiculed and aspects of religion criticized.
The *gharbzada* (Westomaniac) had replaced Nasr al-Din and Hajji Baba
as the favorite target of social critics. However, it is in the realm of
political culture that the survival, revival, or "return" of the sacred is
most noticeable.

In democratic societies, when the public gets tired of a party that
has remained in power too long and has lost its original promise of
political renewal, it turns to another party, even if this means switching
to a rival one and forsaking an old party alignment. In a country like
Iran, in contrast, dissatisfaction with the established regime leads to a
search for a new "identity" that entails not merely a change in political
party membership, but a revision or even replacement of belief systems.
Current trends in lay and clerical Islamic ideologies demonstrate how
historical change forces upon society this task of revision.

Popular novelists and essayists sought authenticity in their Islamic
culture, which they opposed to the Pahlavis' policy of glorification of
the pre-Islamic heritage. Furthermore, they developed an anti-Western,

aggressively self-defensive nationalist attitude that denounced gharb-zadagi as the root of all social and political ills of the country. Religious tradition became the measure of their ideological separateness from the official order. They appealed to both the tradition-bound lower classes, who felt betrayed and powerless vis-à-vis the gharbzada, and the Western-educated. "The root of my tradition is Islamic," wrote Jalal Al-e Ahmad;[7] "Islam is the only traditional bond that strongly unifies the nation," wrote 'Alireza Maibodi;[8] "the Islamic culture is the only culture that is still alive today," wrote 'Ali Shari'ati.[9] All three were speaking not of the Islam of the ulama, but of a rejuvenated, reformed, and, in the case of Shari'ati, ideologized Islam. They referred to the spirit of the Hidden Imam as a source of spiritual inspiration and moral strength, yet they conceived the intellectual as the "prophet" of the age, the "torchbearer," the guide, the leader. The intellectual would renew religion, make it a viable force to combat the "cultural imperialism" of the West and dictatorship at home and, more important, to awaken society from the centuries-long stupor inflicted by traditional religion. In Shari'ati's works the Imam is depicted not as a martyr, but as a conquering hero, a radical activist, and *entezar* (the Shi'i expectation of the Imam's return) is turned into expectation of earthly perfection to be realized through revolutionary action. With Shari'ati, the Western-educated sociologist, entezar became inseparable from historical determinism. It is part of the messianic faith, he wrote, to believe in the "return of the Golden Age," in the revolution that will bring it about, and in the reign of peace and justice on earth. Entezar is thus part of a "future-oriented" ideology opposed to "backward-looking" traditionalism.[10]

Khomeini's conception of the Imamate likewise strips it of its element of pathos and transforms it into a concrete model for Islamic government. The Imamate retains its eschatological nature but is more graphically invoked to provide legitimacy to the new theory of government. I have stated elsewhere[11] that, paradoxical as it may seem, Khomeini can best be understood as a man of his time and his revolution as a stage in, rather than a reaction to, modernization. I have argued that his theory of the *velayat-e faqih* (the governance of the jurist) constitutes a radical departure from the classical Shi'a Islamic view of government, showing how, in his innovative interpretation of traditional religious texts, politics displaces theology and political goals acquire priority over doctrinal concerns. Indeed, he has attempted to break the nation's ties to the religio-political culture in which it has been reared and to replace it with, not an old belief system, but a reinterpreted, ideologized conception of the old system.

In contrast to Shari'ati's and other lay Islamic ideologists' conception of the *raushanfekr* (intellectual), Khomeini's *faqih* lays claim to absolute authority as the representative of the Imam, and his task is to restore the rule of Islamic law conceived as universal and immutable. He uses the terms *qanun* (earlier used for 'orf law and then for constitutional government decrees) and shar' interchangeably, thereby expressing his rejection of the traditional distinction of public from Islamic law. Indeed, his conception of Islamic law is different from the traditional Muslim view. His notion that divine law and human law are mutually exclusive is contradicted by the practical development of the law in Muslim countries. Moreover, instead of limiting his expertise to legal matters and accommodating temporal government, Khomeini attributes to the faqih all the political rights of the Imams and the Prophet and demands complete obedience to his rule. He thus chooses the esotericists' concept of a single source of authority and reverses the jurists' traditional preference for collective leadership. He grants legitimacy to his theory of the governance of the jurist by unequivocally declaring the faqih the rightful successor to the Imams. His claims go far beyond Nai'ini's cautious phrasing of his support for the constitutional form of government as the least offensive to the doctrine of the Imamate since, by definition, all governments amount to usurpation of the Imam's right to rule. Khomeini's claims also represent an extreme version of Mostafa Ansari's view of velayat-e faqih. The nineteenth-century jurist seems to have been the first Shi'i theologian to use this terminology, but he carefully qualified his stand by acknowledging ekhtelaf and noting the tradition of accommodation.[12]

The constitution of the Islamic Republic has abolished monarchy as un-Islamic and thus granted legitimacy to a form of government that was rejected by the leading mojtaheds of the 1920s. Provisions that Nuri and fellow opponents of the 1906 constitution denounced as contrary to Islam are incorporated in the new one. The Islamic constitution, on the other hand, includes things not even deemed worthy of consideration at the turn of the century, such as granting women the right to vote and even to be elected to the Majlis. What aroused controversy then no longer stirs a ripple in the religious circles of today. Social change has imposed recognition of what was conceived in the past as "unorthodox," "heretical," or emulation of the mores of the "infidels." Might continued historical change further alter Shi'i views and theories?

Shi'a Islam had consistently avoided any attempt at providing a universal definition of the legitimate state in the absence of the Imam. The concept of the velayat-e faqih has yet to be fully accepted by all ulama and incorporated into the doctrine of ghaiba. So far the high-ranking religious scholars of Shi'a Islam outside Iran have remained hostile to it. Within Iran doctrinal debates are not allowed, as the recent silencing of the Anjoman-e Hojjatiyya has shown. This organization, founded in the shah's time, was primarily involved in religious propaganda against Marxism and Baha'ism. It reportedly became highly influential within the ruling circles in 1981–83, recruiting its members from within the Majlis, the Council of Guardians, and the cabinet and among wealthy landowners. It consistently opposed the theory of the governance of the jurist; espousing the traditional Twelver Shi'a view of the Hidden Imam as the sole righteous ruler, it argued against clerical assumption of temporal rule.

In the summer of 1983 Khomeini, in a speech marking the end of Ramadan (the month of fasting), attacked the traditional belief that corruption must reign supreme until it reaches its paroxysm and thus hastens the return of the Imam. "Why is the Twelfth Imam returning?" he asked. "He is returning in order to wipe out sins. Should we then commit sins in order for him to return?" He asked his audience to "keep away from such falsehoods and deceits" and threatened the Anjoman's members, without mentioning names, with "having their hands and feet broken." In response to Khomeini's speech, the Anjoman announced the suspension of its activities and professed its willingness to work to preserve unity and confront the evil influence of "foreign propaganda" and the "enemies of Islam." Neither Khomeini nor the speakers in the Majlis nor the press offered any theological counterargument to the Anjoman's views or cited any religious texts as evidence of the validity of their own stand. In fact, the campaign against the Anjoman is political in nature. Its members are denounced as having been officials of SAVAK and other agencies of the Pahlavi regime. They are linked to the Mojahedin opposition. They are called "reactionary" and "antirevolutionary," since they view any political movement before the return of the Twelfth Imam as religious innovation. A Majlis deputy went so far as to accuse them of affiliation with the Wahabis (the Sunni fundamentalist sect to which the reigning House of Saud in Arabia adheres) and of not being true followers of the Hidden Imam. Since the Anjoman is reportedly opposed to nationalization of trade and redistribution of land, it has been held responsible for the hoarding of food and inflationary prices.[13] Thus, it has been used as a scapegoat for the severe shortage of basic commodities.

Whether the theory of the governance of the jurist will survive Khomeini remains to be seen. The novelty of the ulama's dual function, temporal and spiritual, underscores the precariousness of their self-proclaimed right to rule. As Khomeini himself recently remarked, now that, for the first time in Islamic history, the ulama are entrusted with the "responsibility" of protecting Islam, they must be careful to prevent the erosion of their credibility and their prestige. "Should we ever, God forbid, alienate the nation from ourselves as a result of our deeds, we would have to answer their questions as to why we have failed in our duty to protect Islam, and why we have not acted accordingly. The enemies of Islam would then triumphantly take over from us."[14] Khomeini identifies Islam with the ulama and pronounces the ulama's enemies Islam's enemies. His followers repeatedly chant slogans implying that he rules by divine right and proclaiming that cognizance of the Hidden Imam is possible only through love of Khomeini. Nevertheless, Khomeini and other ruling religious scholars recognize the right of the "nation" (*mellat*) to judge them should they err and the potential threat of popular uprisings against their regime.

The cult of the Hidden Imam has survived social and political upheavals and has often outgrown official religious policies intolerant of deviations from orthodoxy. Throughout the long history of the sect, Shi'a believers have been able to renew their individual understanding of and faith in the Imamate, divorced from temporal politics. The religious controversies that divided the ranks of the religious establishment in premodern Iran and that lost their vitality as a result of the secularization of the educational system now threaten to resurface. In response to the Islamic Revolution, Iranian young people are increasingly showing interest in Islamic history and culture. Their perception of their religious heritage is bound to reflect their openness to modern life-styles and the geographical and social mobility they now enjoy. Their discussion of the social issues of the day may display a heightened self-awareness resulting from their having experienced a revolution that toppled a power structure until then viewed as invincible and omnipotent. The crisis of self-consciousness arising from a possible loss of faith in clerical government, if not accompanied by a loss in religious certitude, could lead to a serious challenge to the present ideologized interpretation of the doctrine of the Imamate. The most vigorous challenge could come not from within the ranks of the religious establishment, as it did in premodern Iran, but from without.

Notes

1. Norman Calder, "Accommodation and Revolution in Imami Shi'i Jurisprudence: Khumayni and the Classical Tradition," *Middle Eastern Studies* 18 (1982):4.

2. Mangol Bayat, *Mysticism and Dissent: Socioreligious Thought in Qajar Iran* (Syracuse: Syracuse University Press, 1982).

3. *al-Jamal* (Tehran, n.d.), nos. 17, 18, 23.

4. *Tanbih al-Omma va Tanzih al-Mella*, 3d ed., with an introduction and annotation by Sayyed Mahmud Talaqani (Tehran, 1955).

5. See Abdul-Hadi Hairi, *Shi'ism and Constitutionalism in Iran* (Leiden, 1977).

6. Daniel Bell, "The Return of the Sacred?" in *The Winding Passage: Essays and Sociological Journeys* (New York, 1980), p. 332.

7. Jalal Al-Ahmad, *Arzyabi-ye Shetabzada* (Tabriz, 1965), p. 89.

8. 'Alireza Maibodi, *Raushanfekran: Tarek-e Donya* (Shiraz, 1973), p. 47.

9. Ali Shari'ati, *Bazgasht be Khishtan*, transcript of the lecture at Ahvaz University, n.d., English translation by M. Bayat in *Islam in Transition: Muslim Perspectives*, ed. John D. Donohue and John L. Esposito (New York, 1982), pp. 305–7.

10. "Entezar," in *Madhhab-e E'teraz* (Tehran, 1971).

11. M. Bayat, "The Iranian Revolution of 1978–79: Fundamentalist or Modern?" *Middle East Journal* 37, no. 1 (1983).

12. Calder, "Accommodation and Revolution."

13. *Iran Times*, August 12 and 19, 1983.

14. *Iran Times*, June 17, 1983.

WILLIAM L. HANAWAY, JR.

The Symbolism of
Persian Revolutionary Posters

The symbolism of a corpus of twenty-nine posters collected in Iran up to 1979 represents two profoundly differing world views and views of the Islamic Revolution.* Without proposing a theory of symbolism, I will say briefly what I mean by a symbol in this context. Here I follow Dan Sperber to some extent. Persons can be said to have two kinds of knowledge: that which can be made explicit and thus learned by rote and that which cannot. This latter is "tacit" knowledge and has as its data "intuitions . . . judgements that members of a culture group systematically express without elaborating on the underlying argument."[1] Symbols evoke this tacit knowledge. A symbol stands in a metaphoric relationship to the tacit knowledge that it evokes and, consequently, may be unintelligible by itself. A metaphoric relationship is one based on an arbitrary assertion of similarity. The association of A and B may be arbitrary but habitual, thus giving the impression that it has some natural or organic basis (the serpent as a symbol of evil in Western art, for example), or it may be arbitrary and private, as in the symbols appearing in dreams or in poems. In neither case is there an intrinsic relationship between A and B.

A symbol and its interpretation are not a closed, restrictive pair such as signified and signifier in language. The symbol is not to be compared to the word; rather, as Sperber says, it is a "landmark" that organizes our experience.[2] Every individual's experience is unique, though determined in many ways by his culture. Thus there must be a degree of latitude in the relationship of symbol and interpretation, not a one-to-one correspondence. The tacit knowledge evoked by a symbol will never

---

*These posters were first displayed at Long Island University in December 1982 and were presented again at the Brooklyn College conference at which the paper was read. I thank Susan Kinsey, Youssef M. Ibrahim, Ervand Abrahamian, and James F. Hitselberger for their generosity in allowing me access to their collections of posters.

be absolutely determined, and the individual will have a measure of freedom in this respect. This is because a symbol organizes our experience by focusing our tacit knowledge, and since symbols may be cross-cultural, this focusing may have a cross-cultural dimension. What is specific to a given culture is the symbol's evocational field.

Marshall Segall makes the point that our experiences combine in a complex fashion to influence how we react to any stimulus situation. Our experience is determined by our culture, and therefore, in Segall's words, "visual experiences most generally available in a particular environment predispose one to identify most readily materials similar to the content of those experiences."[3] Thus there is more to seeing than meets the eye. Cultural symbols need not be totally inaccessible to outsiders, however. I am not Iranian, but I have studied and thought about Iranian culture. I am, no doubt, predisposed to perceive stimuli in a manner determined by my own past cultural experience, but this experience includes a measure of Iranian as well as American culture. To what extent the tacit knowledge evoked in me by the symbolism of these posters corresponds to an Iranian's response remains to be seen.

The posters of the corpus fall into two groups in terms of their symbolism, subject matter, and style. One group consists of graphic designs with many elements common to revolutionary posters the world over. The other includes portraits of Ayatollah Khomeini done in various styles and designs derived from indigenous Persian painting. The range of pictorial styles, iconographic content, and implied world views in these posters is very broad. These variations, I suggest, are worth discussing at some length because they reflect some of the main political and intellectual preoccupations of the revolutionary forces.

The extensive use of posters for political purposes began in the nineteenth century, but it was the Russian Revolution in 1917 that made the poster an important means of communicating a revolutionary message to the people. At the same time, the Russian revolutionary poster artists developed themes and symbols that have become part of the standard visual repertoire of the genre.[4] During the revolution in Cuba against the government of Fulgencio Batista, posters came into their own both as artistic creations and as a means of communicating revolution to the world. Long after Fidel Castro had assumed power, posters continued to be used by the Cuban government for social as well as political messages, stressing, for example, the need to conserve electricity, the importance of literacy, or the need for every citizen to work hard to achieve a record sugarcane harvest.

Cuba exported not only revolution (if we are to believe some national leaders) but also revolutionary poster art. In 1970 and 1971 Cuban artists prepared a number of posters celebrating Third World solidarity congresses and similar events. These posters combined native cultural symbols with the international revolutionary ones and carried messages in the languages of the people to whom they were addressed. For example, there were several posters aimed at Palestinians, showing Arab symbols and motifs, revolutionary symbols such as guns and raised fists, and messages in Arabic. I have seen no examples designed for Iranians, but it is certainly possible that these Cuban exports provided models for some of the international-style Persian posters made around 1979.[5]

The international-style graphic posters use bold, formalized designs in few colors. With three exceptions, these posters have messages in Persian and English, including dates and the names of the designer and the producer. The inscriptions are generally as integral a part of the design of the poster as the label on a pair of designer jeans.

The first poster is entitled "Azadi-ye Qalam—For A Free Press," dated "Mehr '57" (October–November 1978) (see Figure 1). Two rifles form two sides of a triangle, at the apex of which is the head of a stylized dove holding a rose in its beak. The bird's body forms the lower part of the design, and its neck makes a complicated coil up through the center of the triangle. The bird appears to have been shot with the rifles; heart-shaped drops of blood drip from its head. The names of the artist and the producer appear prominently in English and Persian. This design combines three important elements of what may be called the international repertoire of revolutionary symbols. The design itself probably derives from a Cuban poster of 1970 showing two rifles arranged in a similar triangle. Guns, flowers, and doves are clichés of revolutionary art, as are screaming faces, prisoners in striped uniforms, marching workers, and raised fists. Here the designer has adapted the dove to his theme of freedom of the press by making the bird's body and head resemble the nib of a pen.[6]

A poster entitled "Baraye Emruz—For Today," dated "Aban '57— Oct. '78," is said to commemorate the massacre of students at the University of Tehran. Here four screaming faces in black are composed with four red rifles, each pointing into a mouth, and one red rifle linking the two pairs of figures. A bold black calligraphic design ties the whole composition together.[7]

Dated in the same month is a poster called "Payanda Iran—Long Live Iran," showing five blindfolded, screaming prisoners in striped prison uniforms standing against brick walls with their hands tied behind their backs, the whole overlain by nineteen small black rifles. A wedge of white through the waist of each figure gives a sense of imminent

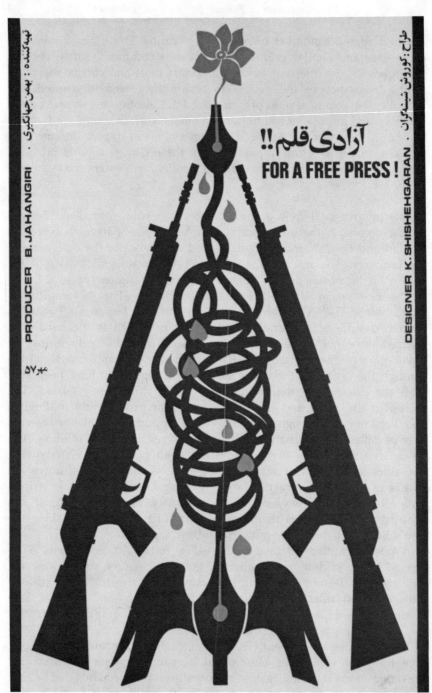

Figure 1. "For a Free Press."

collapse. The design employs the simple principle of repetition, using rifles and screaming prisoners, to convey its message.[8]

Two posters commemorate the massacre in Zhala Square which took place on 17 Shahrivar 1357/Friday, October 8, 1978. The first, called "Jom'e-ye Siyah—Black Friday," shows eight corpses wrapped in shrouds, with a red rifle and a red-and-black inscription on each. Here the background is black to set off the white shrouds, and simple repetition is the only device used.[9] The second seems to be a photograph of a street sign for Zhala Square set on a brick wall, with a picture of Khomeini taped to the sign and a handprint and inscription over it saying (in Persian) "God Is Great. The Martyrs of the 17th of Shahrivar."[10] Pictures of walls, usually with photographic clarity, are commonplaces of revolutionary poster art.

The only poster of this group dedicated to an individual is one dated Bahman 1357/February 1979 showing a profile of Mohammad Mosaddeq. The former prime minister's face and head are plastered with red, white, and green bandages, suggesting the Persian flag. Mosaddeq is facing and pointing to the left, and there are seven small red rifles around his hand also pointing left, giving a strong leftward movement to the design. The interesting thing about this poster is that it contains a quotation from Hafez: "I am the slave of the Magian elder who will free me from ignorance."[11] The image of the Magian elder, presumably meant to refer to Mosaddeq himself, suggests a complex of images appearing in the amatory-mystical *ghazal* tradition of Persian classical poetry. The Magian elder is Iranian but not Muslim and is a source of divine guidance to those who seek his aid.[12]

In the same month (February 1979) there appeared another poster entitled "Diruz. Emruz. (Farda)?—Yesterday. Today. (Tomorrow)?" (See the jacket cover of this volume.) It shows a calligraphic figure representing Iran or an Iranian being squeezed in a vise made of two opposed pistols labeled with a U.S. flag and a red flag bearing a white question mark. The vise is labeled (in Persian) "Imperialism."[13]

In March 1979, the Writers' Association issued a poster showing a man and a woman, with screaming faces, in shrouds bound with red rope. The only caption is a large question mark between the figures; the date is given in English and Persian.[14]

May Day of 1979 produced two posters in this collection. In these the symbolism moves away from the specifically Iranian to the international, with no clear Iranian association except in the inscriptions, which are in Persian only. The first shows faceless workers marching toward the viewer with arms linked. The text says "The Eleventh of Ordibehesht [The First of May]. Let us celebrate as splendidly as possible the World Day of the Worker. Workers of Iran, unite." The line of marching workers breaks through the margins of the picture and gives an impression of great numbers.[15] The other poster uses other revolutionary clichés: two hands grasping a wrench, a hammer, and a red flower. The legend says "The Eleventh of Ordibehesht. World Workers' Day."[16]

A much more imaginative use of a common symbol is a poster showing a dove shattered into many pieces. The incription says "Paranda-ye Azadi!!—Bird of Freedom!! Khordad '58—May '79."[17]

The last two posters of this group are undated. One seems to reflect attitudes common during the summer and fall of 1979. It shows the symbol of the University of Tehran with American footprints on it. The legend is "Farhang-e Amrika'i Ekhraj Bayad Gardad—Iranian Universities Are the Bases of Imperialism." Here, untypically, the English is not a translation of the Persian, which is "American Culture Must Be Expelled."[18] The last poster shows a collage of communication equipment: a typewriter keyboard and Telex machines beneath a map of the world. A white sheet of paper emerging from a machine is folded over and becomes black. Concentric circles move outward from the center of the picture. The caption begins with a quotation, in Arabic and Persian, from Quran 49:6: "O believers, if an ungodly man comes to you with a tiding, make clear." At the bottom, in Persian, is "Islamic Republican Party. On the Occasion of the March Protesting Zionist News Reporting."

In the second group of posters, the eight portraits of Khomeini derive their designs from sources as varied as Cuban portraits of Fidel Castro and Che Guevara and Italian Baroque madonnas. Khomeini is always shown in religious garb, and this is true of representations of him in other posters of the collection as well. This consistency contrasts with the various ways in which the shah appeared in the pictures of him that were so common before the revolution. While the shah, using a Western political technique, tried to appeal to different groups by dressing as a pilgrim, a Boy Scout, a businessman, or a military leader, Khomeini always looks the same: unchanging, clear of purpose, and single-minded. Although it is probably true that Khomeini always does dress this way in daily life, the contrast with the portraits of the shah is clear, as is the parallel with portraits of Castro and Guevara, who always appear in military dress.

The simplest portraits of Khomeini show only his head and shoulders and have no verbal messages other than his name. In one case this is in English and Persian in a stylized script resembling computer-readable type; in another it is in a decorative Arabic script. The latter has a red-and-green background, suggesting the colors of the Iranian flag. Next is a portrait in the Cuban style with Khomeini's face against a red background and two messages on land reform, one his own and the other from Ayatollah Montazeri.[19] The last of the straightforward representations is a photograph of Khomeini, without his turban, in the midst of a crowd. Surrounding the photograph is a montage of newspaper headlines quoting him on the need for national unity.

The remaining four are portraits of Khomeini in symbolic contexts. These all derive from a painterly tradition and carry somewhat more complex messages. One shows him holding a Quran in his left hand and raising his right hand to acknowledge the greetings of a large crowd. Surrounding him are representative individuals from all walks of Persian society: peasants, laborers, soldiers and officers, white-collar workers, and intellectuals. Of the thirteen persons most prominently displayed, six are women (all with heads covered), and one woman is as high in the picture as Khomeini himself. Above the ayatollah, upon whom a bright ray of sunshine falls, are two angels, one blowing a trumpet to mark the occasion. The symbolism here derives from Russian socialist-realist painting. The emphasis is on the leader and the masses, and individuals other than the leader become representative types. To the Western eye the suggestion of Khomeini as Christ is clear.

An enigmatic portrait shows Khomeini full-figure with the sun directly behind his head, forming a bright halo. Six large flowers looking like dandelions gone to seed are backlighted by the sun, but Khomeini's face and the garments under his black robe are also strongly lighted, although turned away from the sun. The ambiguous light sources and the unusually large flowers prevent this poster from communicating a clear message. Clearer, at least to the Western eye, is the message of a portrait of Khomeini deriving directly from an Italian Baroque painting of the Madonna. Here we see the ayatollah standing on a stone with a serpent curling around his feet. In a turbulent sky in the background, cherubim gaze upon him from four positions in the clouds. A dove hovers over his head, and a cherub at his feet carries red tulips. Below Khomeini, who is dressed in a blue robe, are a fallen tree and a fallen slab.

It is striking to see Khomeini substituting for the Virgin Mary in a portrait the formal organization and iconography of which are quite remote from the Iranian tradition. A blue robe, for example, is characteristic of the Madonna in Baroque painting, but not of Khomeini in portraits. On closer consideration, however, the poster begins to make more sense. To begin with, it must be viewed in the context of the Islamic Revolution in Tehran. Certain of its elements would have been echoed in other posters seen around town at the same time. For example, the dove over Khomeini's head in the Baroque model for this portrait is a symbol of the Holy Spirit, but in the present context we must see it as an international symbol of peace. It appears in other posters in this collection and is part of the standard repertoire of international political symbols.

An element that must be seen in its Persian context is the bunch of tulips held by the cherub at Khomeini's feet. The tulip (*lala*) has long been associated in Iran with love and death. Numerous verses in Ferdausi's *Shahnama* compare the color of blood to the color of the tulip.[20] In early texts the tulip was also called *no'man,* which in Arabic means "blood," and sometimes *shaqa'eq al-no'man,* which today means "anemone." An Arabic legend from Lebanon and Syria says that anemones grew from the spilled blood of Adonis.[21] A parallel legend in the *Shahnama* concerns Siyavosh, the perfect youth who was unjustly killed by Afrasiyab, king of Turan: "Immediately a plant grew from that blood/ Only God knows how that plant grew/ I will point out that plant to you now/ It is called 'The Blood of Siyavosh.' "[22] Siyavosh was killed because he would not compromise his honesty and is therefore considered a martyr. The red flower that grew from his blood was a sign of his martyrdom, and this flower was identified with the tulip.

There is evidence indicating that the notion of martyrdom was important in Iranian culture before the coming of Islam. Wall paintings excavated at Panjikent in Sogdiana show what seems to be a mourning procession, and this has been interpreted as a ceremony commemorating the death of Siyavosh.[23] There is no need to expand on what the martyrdom of Imam Hosain means to Shi'i Iranians. Records of mourning processions on 'Ashura, the anniversary of Hosain's death, go back at least to the Buyid period, and after 1500 these ceremonies became more and more elaborate, always focused on the central fact of martyrdom. When supporters of Khomeini were killed in the revolutionary struggle against the Pahlavi regime, Khomeini declared them martyrs. The tulip appeared very early in the revolution as a symbol of those who gave their lives in the cause of overthrowing the shah. For example, a militant poem by Khosrau Golesorkhi entitled "Tulips of My City" uses the tulip to stand for the young men of Tehran who are ready to sacrifice themselves fighting the shah.[24] Another example occurs in a 1979 song by Hamid Hamza called "Unity": "O tulip lying in mud and blood/ The horizons became red from your blood."[25]

The tulip is also metaphorically associated with love and beauty. Specifically, it is a common image for the cheek of the beloved. An example from Ferdausi is "His two eyes are sleepy and his face re-splendent/ His cheek is filled with tulips and his hair with musk."[26] Examples from Hafez show how the aspects of love and death in tulip imagery combine: "Maybe your heart will become aware of my state/ When tulips grow from the tombs of those who died from love of you"[27] and "I still see how, from longing for Shirin's lips/ Tulips grow from Farhad's bloody tears."[28]

In the context of revolutionary posters, poems, and songs, the richness of the tulip as a symbol derives from its power to link the Iranian and the Islamic heritages in Persian culture and, in Sperber's terms, to evoke the tacit knowledge that every Iranian has of an event carrying powerful religious and national significance.

The painter of the poster under discussion had undoubtedly been trained in Europe in the beaux arts tradition and had probably copied pictures like this in his classes. He must have had some idea of the religious significance of the scene. By substituting Khomeini for the Virgin Mary and making some small iconographic changes, he could preserve many elements of the style and formal composition of the Italian model while portraying Khomeini in a more blatantly religious context than would have been possible in a painting in the traditional Iranian style. This sort of Baroque madonna almost always contained a dove and often lilies, the latter easily converted into tulips. By using well-known revolutionary symbols as elements of the design, the painter created a work that shared two cultures. He could exploit Western symbolism by putting it to the service of the Eastern revolution.

The last of the Khomeini portraits also uses tulips. A wounded woman holding a child struggles down a road toward the horizon, over which hovers a dominating image of Khomeini against a dark sky. On the road directly ahead of her, huge tulips burst through the asphalt. The tarred road across the desert is shattered by the flowers growing from the blood of martyrs. The woman's blood links her with the tulips which destroy the Western-style highway built from Persian oil, a *shahrah* that leads to a dead end at Khomeini.[29]

Two posters that do not fit easily with the others will be mentioned here. One shows a student musing at a graveside. On the gravestone is the picture of another youth, and in the dark clouds above can be seen vague, grief-stricken faces that may represent a younger sister, an older brother, and other relatives. The youth is wearing Keds. The other poster is done in a realistic style and shows a woman with two small children ministering to a wounded soldier in a bunker, while in the distance a battle involving tanks and warplanes rages. A large white band at the bottom, not at all integrated with the design, has a quotation from Khomeini, in Persian: "Today is the day when it is incumbent on the entire nation to offer close and necessary cooperation with the soldiers and guardians of Islam and Iran." These posters represent two aspects of the struggle in which the Iranians are currently engaged, one against themselves and one against the Iraqis. Two sorts of pain that result from violence are depicted, the mental and the physical. Neither poster uses the international symbols of the graphic posters or the Iranian and Islamic symbols of the posters to be discussed below.

The final group consists of six posters which feature Khomeini, the shah, and scenes from the revolution in styles that derive from traditional coffeehouse paintings and classical manuscript illustrations. The first shows a group of young Iranians surrounded by dead bodies, raising a flag which says (in Arabic) "There is no God but God." On the right an equestrian statue is being pulled down, and in the background tanks defend large, modern buildings. Hovering over the buildings and dominating the entire scene is Khomeini, his fist raised. A number of red arrows in the upper part of the picture, possibly representing the souls of the martyrs in the foreground, point toward heaven. Here Khomeini appears as the driving force behind the revolution.

A poster showing the shah at the mouth of hell very skillfully links Iranian and Islamic symbols (see Figure 2). The setting is a mountainous, forested area, probably Mazandaran. The composition is divided neatly in half: balancing the mouth of hell on the right are the sun and the face of Khomeini on the left. Half of the sun is visible above the horizon. An angel with a white body and wings, dark hair and eyes, and a human face flies in the sky near the ayatollah. The shah is slumped at the mouth of hell with his crown under his arm; gold coins and thousand-dollar bills leak from his suitcase. Within hell, the devil holds up a sign saying (in Persian) "Welcome to Hell." Over the heads of former officials standing in the flames (including Amir 'Abbas Hoveida with his pipe) is a banner saying "We honor the visit of our great master to hell. The Society of Devils of Hell." The language of this banner imitates the formal style used on banners in cities and towns when the shah would pay an official visit. Each official wears a sign saying "Corrupter on Earth."

The scene has strong overtones of the story of Zahhak from the *Shahnama*. Zahhak was an evil usurper whose most prominent characteristic was two snakes that grew from his shoulders and that required human brains as their daily sustenance. After many years Zahhak was overthrown by Feridun, and he fled. When he was finally captured, he was taken to Mt. Damavand and hung upside-down in a cave deep under the mountain, to remain there until the end of time. Damavand is a volcano and has long been important in Iranian mythology. In the poster the forested, mountainous terrain, the fire inside the mountain, and the deposed shah with a snake on either side of him all suggest the story of Zahhak. At the same time Khomeini, the angel, and the sinners burning in hell establish the Islamic dimensions of the scene, and the two traditions are perfectly integrated. The yellow, rising sun

Figure 2. "Welcome to Hell."

suggests the ascending new order and is balanced by the round, red mouth of hell symbolizing the descent into darkness of the old regime.

A poster with a simpler message shows Khomeini holding a Quran and dominating a panorama of Tehran in which two events are taking place. Behind the ayatollah is a green banner with the following quotation from Quran 17:83, the italicized words of which are visible: "And say: *'The truth has come, and falsehood has vanished away;* surely falsehood is ever certain to vanish.'" Above Khomeini's head can be read "God Is Great" and Quran 3:163, "Count not those who were slain in God's way as dead, but rather living with their Lord, by Him provided," in Arabic and Persian. The right-hand scene shows the rally of two million people on December 10, 1978, calling for the establishment of an Islamic republic. The rally was held at the Shahyad monument, built by the shah to celebrate twenty-five hundred years of Iranian kingship. The left-hand scene shows the massacre in Zhala Square on Black Friday, September 8, 1978. The Quranic quotations apply appropriately to the events depicted.[30]

A second poster by the same artist shows many similarities in detail and composition (see Figure 3). Here again is Khomeini with a Quran and a green banner saying "Islamic Republic" on one side and "There Is No God But God" on the other. "God Is Great" is written in the sky. Khomeini looks down over a map of Iran from approximately the location of the Caspian Sea, and the shah is seen in Saudi Arabia, having just crossed the Persian Gulf from Iran. The monarch, accompanied by a small dog and a devil (cf. Quran 43:36: "Whoso blinds himself to the Remembrance of the All-Merciful, to him We assign a Satan for comrade"), runs bareheaded toward the West spilling gold coins and paper money from two handbags adorned with British and American flags. The British bag says "$165 Billion." The right side of the picture shows the Eiffel Tower and an airplane heading away from it toward a mosque, symbolizing the return of Khomeini from France. Important events in the revolution are depicted on the map, including the shooting of the students at the University of Tehran, the burning of the Rex Cinema in Abadan, the rally of two million in Tehran, various events in Tabriz, Zanjan, and Qazvin, and the execution of former high officials of the shah's government, labeled "Corrupters on Earth." The abundance of detail in these two posters, the simultaneous presence of a number of scenes taking place at different times, the emphasis on the role of powerful persons, the lack of perspective, the lack of redundancy, and the frequent use of labels all link this style of painting to traditional coffeehouse paintings, particularly ones showing the events at Karbala.

The last two posters, with one that has appeared elsewhere,[31] form an iconographically and symbolically unified group. Closer to the style

Figure 3. Exit the shah, enter Khomeini.

of classical miniatures than to coffeehouse paintings, these posters show Khomeini as Moses, holding a scroll or pointing to a Quranic verse, and the shah, representing the pharaoh, being attacked by a fiery serpent. Combining Iranian and Islamic symbolism, one poster shows the ayatollah holding up a scroll that says "God Is Great." He is located in the heavens, and rays of strong light come from behind him. The shah is a small figure in the foreground, fleeing toward a fire-breathing dragon while being attacked from above by a huge bird of prey in the shape of Iran. Again the shah has crossed the Persian Gulf and is in a wasteland. Above and below the bird are written (in Persian) "Caspian Sea" and "Persian Gulf," and in the upper left-hand part of the picture is a quotation from 'Ali b. Abi Taleb, in Arabic: "The lowest among you will become the highest, and the highest among you the lowest." This is accompanied by an expanded interpretation in Persian. The bird of prey may be intended to suggest the mythical bird Simorgh, which aids Iranian heroes against their foes.

Khomeini is again shown as Moses the Deliverer in the last poster of this series (see Figure 4). Here again he holds a scroll with the message "God is Great. The secret of the Muslims' victory lies in faith in God and unity of speech." The waters divide diagonally across the picture, with Khomeini on the left shore. Behind him is a cemetery with many graves, and above it is written "Tulips have grown from the blood of the nation's youth." Indeed, a red tulip appears beside each grave. On the right shore of the sea, against the columns of Persepolis, lies the shah, bareheaded, his crown and sword lying shattered beside him. He is being attacked by a fiery dragon, and beneath his leg is written "Anyone who tries to blow out a lamp lighted by God will burn his beard."

In all three of these posters the dragon represents the staff of Moses that was turned into a snake by God as a demonstration of his power. In post-Quranic legend the snake sometimes becomes a dragon, and two of the characteristics of dragons in Persian popular lore are that they breathe fire and that they are able to draw their prey toward their maw simply by inhaling. Here the dragon lies across the waters of the sea, its tail near the cemetery and its head near the shah. The serpent of the Quranic account is here interpreted according to Iranian popular belief, and it ties the left-hand, "Islamic" side of the picture to the right-hand, "Iranian" side. On the Iranian side we see the pharaoh-shah identified with Persepolis, the symbol of ancient Iran, and both are about to be destroyed by Moses-Khomeini's dragon. While the shah attempts to take refuge in the dead city of the Achaemenids, Khomeini stands by the graveyard of recent martyrs (the graves have names and dates on them). On his side, in addition, are signs of life in the form

Figure 4. Khomeini overwhelms the shah.

of tulips springing from each grave and the border of cypresses that surrounds the graveyard. Here, as in the poster of the shah at the mouth of hell, Islamic and Iranian symbols are completely integrated into a single design that must have been highly suggestive to viewers in revolutionary Tehran.

In considering this collection of posters, some significant contrasts can be seen. For example, in the modern designs, red, white, and black predominate, while in the traditional ones there is a general broadening of the palette and green is much in evidence. Green is an important color in Islam. It is believed that the Prophet's banner and 'Ali's cloak were green. In *ta'ziya* (religious drama) performances in Iran, the actor playing Hosain always wears green, and popular paintings of the Shi'i martyrs, Joseph, Solomon, and other admired figures are generally dressed in green. Red, black, and white, on the other hand, are the dominant colors in the Russian revolutionary posters mentioned above and are characteristic of left-wing revolutionary posters from other parts of the world.

As for the designs themselves, the modern ones are generally hard-edged, with relatively little detail and a good deal of redundancy. Individuals are depersonalized and reduced to types, and there is often an impression of photographic clarity. These characteristics suggest a connection with Western advertising art, and especially a type of advertising poster, seen less often these days than formerly, that uses a strong, simple design and bold colors to communicate a simple message rapidly. The photographic quality of the posters suggests to the viewer that what he is seeing is true, for "the camera does not lie." We know, of course, that this is not the case and that the eye does not see as the camera lens sees. Nevertheless the illusion persists, and photographs were widely used on posters by opposition groups within and outside Iran during the revolutionary period.

The traditional posters tend to be representations rather than symbolic designs. They contain lots of detail and little redundancy: i.e., every element in the picture means something and contributes to a complex message. The persons depicted, usually Khomeini and the shah, are easily recognizable and individualized. These qualities tie this group of posters to the indigenous traditions of coffeehouse painting and manuscript illustration. Coffeehouse paintings often have an abundance of detail and frequently display together a number of different events that occurred over a period of time. Individuals in these paintings are recognizable because of standard iconographic features or particular attributes, as in paintings of Christian saints. For these reasons, figures that may never have existed, such as Rostam, are easily identifiable in Persian paintings.

The use of writing in these posters is consistent with the artistic traditions from which they derive. In the modern-style posters the writing is usually an integral part of the design, as is the case with Western advertising designs and contemporary T-shirt art. The message is usually simple, dates are often given in order to focus attention more directly on the message, and the artist's name may be a part of the design. The use of English in these posters directs the message to a certain segment of Persian society, in much the same way that advertisements in the *New Yorker* may use phrases in French while advertisements in *Popular Mechanics* probably will not.

The traditional-style posters, in contrast, do not use writing as a design element except in the case of banners or scrolls held by Khomeini. The writing is simply added to the finished picture, as was the writing in coffeehouse paintings. The written messages tend to be more complicated in these posters than in the modern-style ones, reflecting, in part, a text-based didactic tradition. Finally, the use of Arabic instead of English assumes quite different things about the viewers to whom the message is directed. It is probably safe to say that at the time of the revolution a larger proportion of the population of Tehran and other large cities (excluding Qom) could read and understand English than could read and understand Arabic.

Regarding subject matter, the modern-style posters focus on individual events or single ideas. May Day is commemorated, as is the massacre in Zhala Square, and the only poster focusing on an individual is the commemorative poster for Mohammad Mosaddeq. Even here, however, the picture of Mosaddeq is a design, not a portrait. Ideas such as workers' solidarity or the horrors of war are communicated by the posters, but the emphasis is strongly on the role of events or ideas in history. The individual *qua* recognizable person counts for almost nothing here, as opposed to humans as martyrs or as part of a mass of people. The screaming faces seem to be those of real people but actually are unrecognizable. Instead, they are typical and convey the sense that although the fate of any one person in the revolution may be horrible, larger forces are at work and it takes many martyrs for the revolution to succeed. There is a tension in these posters between their specific message and content and the external traditions of design, language, and symbolism that are invoked to communicate their message. With almost no visual symbolic references to Iranian tradition, these posters internationalize the meaning of the events commemorated. Thus the links with world revolutionary movements and ideologies are more subtle than such clichés as raised fists or workers with linked arms would suggest.

The symbolic message of the traditional-style posters is quite different. Here the emphasis is strongly on powerful individuals and their role in events. History, in these posters, is governed by men, not by ideas. Men, of course, have ideas, but the force of the ideas is concentrated in a man, not in a movement. When specific events are referred to, dates are not given; instead, the events are named or depicted. In the posters in which many things are shown happening at once, however, the figure of Khomeini always dominates the scene and usually stands in polar opposition to a depiction of the shah.

What gives the traditional-style posters a richness of meaning lacking in the modern-style ones is the symbols in them referring to Iranian and Islamic tradition. Some of these posters, such as the one showing Khomeini in the setting of a Baroque madonna, fail in this respect because the symbolic message is ambiguous. The unschooled viewer might not catch the reference to the Virgin Mary, and the pious conservative might resent it. To the Western eye it looks as peculiar as would a nativity scene done in the style of an early Safavid miniature. The schema, to use Gombrich's term, and its contents do not match. In general, however, there is no obvious reference in these posters to an external tradition. Banners with writing on them, inscriptions and labels on the paintings, multiple scenes on one canvas, and a dominating figure all tie these posters to familiar indigenous painting styles. References to Damavand and Zahhak, Moses, and Persepolis are cultural symbols and refer inward.

In the end, two distinct views of the revolution emerge from these comparisons. On the one hand, the Islamic Revolution is linked with larger revolutionary movements and ideas, and its context is at least the Third World if not the entire world. The world to which it is linked in these posters is a humanistic, man-centered world in which men govern themselves by laws that they themselves make. If the modern posters link the present with the future, the traditional ones link the present with the past. In the latter, the revolution is seen as an Iranian and Islamic event, and its context is Iranian history in its sweep from the legendary past to today. It is taking place in a God-centered society in which the rules are divinely given and men are governed by a regent of God. The interplay of these two views as symbolically portrayed in the posters reflects a debate about the Islamic Revolution the long-term resolution of which is by no means clear.

Notes

1. Dan Sperber, *Rethinking Symbolism*, trans. Alice L. Morton (Cambridge: Cambridge University Press, 1975), p. xi.

2. Ibid., p. 33.

3. Marshall Segall, *The Influence of Culture on Visual Perception* (New York: Bobbs-Merrill, 1966), p. 51.

4. See *Posters of the Russian Revolution 1917–1929 from the Lenin Library, Moscow* (New York: Grove Press, 1967).

5. See *Cubaanse Affiches* (Amsterdam: Stedelijk Museum, 1971). In 1980–81 the government of Iran was using posters in the Cuban manner just described. According to a recent article, "the government line is publicized by a flood of posters and wall writings. Posters profusely cover the walls of schools, the mosque, and other public buildings and serve to advertise a large variety of issues, ranging from an appeal to peasants to plant all possible land, to the revolutionary spirit of Islamic women, to the atrocities of American imperialism" ("Current Political Attitudes in an Iranian Village," *Iranian Studies* 16 [1983]:3–29, esp. 23 and 24).

6. Artist: Kurosh Shishagaran. Producer: Bahman Jahangiri. Distributed by the Writers' Association. For a reproduction of the Cuban poster, see Gary Yanker, *Prop Art* (New York: Darien House, 1972), p. 72.

7. Artist: Kurosh Shishagaran. Distributed by the Writers' Association.

8. Artist: Behzad Shishagaran. Distributed by the Writers' Association.

9. Artist: Esma'il Shishagaran. Distributed by the Writers' Association.

10. Distributed by the Army of Guardians of the Islamic Revolution.

11. Hafez, *Divan*, ed. Mohammad Qazvini and Qasem Ghani (Tehran: Zavvar, 1320/1941), p. 108.

12. Artist: Kurosh Shishagaran. Distributed by the Writers' Association.

13. Artist: Kurosh Shishagaran. Distributed by the Writers' Association.

14. Artist: Esma'il Shishagaran.

15. Distributed by left-wing labor unions.

16. Distributed by the Islamic Republican Party. Not reproduced.

17. Artist: Esma'il Shishagaran. Distributed by the Writers' Association. Not reproduced.

18. Sponsored by Islamic Societies and Organizations of Muslim Students in Universities and High Schools of the Country. Distributed by the Reconstruction Crusade.

19. The quotation from Khomeini is "If the laws of Islam are put into effect, nobody will have large landholdings"; the one from Montazeri is "In Islam, the problem of the landlord does not exist." Distributed by the Reconstruction Crusade.

20. See, for example, Ferdausi, *Shahnama*, ed. E. Bertel's et al., 9 vols. (Moscow: Nauka, 1966–71), 2:27, l. 330; 130, l. 62; and 144, l. 267.

21. 'Ali Akbar Dehkhoda, *Loghatnama*, ed. M. Mo'in and J. Shahidi (Tehran: Dehkhoda Organization, 1325/1946–1357/1979), p. 62.

22. Ferdausi, *Shahnama*, 3:152–53, n. 20.

23. Ehsan Yarshater, "Ta'ziyeh and Pre-Islamic Mourning Rites in Iran," in *Ta'ziyeh: Ritual and Drama in Iran*, ed. P. Chelkowski (New York: New York University Press, 1979), pp. 88–94. For reproductions of the wall paintings, see Guitty Azarpay, *Sogdian Painting* (Berkeley: University of California Press, 1981), pp. 128–30.

24. "Lalaha-ye Shahr-e Man," in his *Bargozida-ye Ash'ar* (Tehran: Morvarid, 1358/1979), pp. 71–72.

25. "Ettehad," music by Hosain 'Alizada, on a cassette entitled *Goruh-e Shaida* issued by Chavush.

26. Ferdausi, *Shahnama*, 1:165, 1. 444.

27. Hafez, *Divan*, p. 70.

28. Ibid., p. 65. On the tulip as a symbol in Persian mystical poetry, see Annemarie Schimmel, *As through a Veil: Mystical Poetry in Islam* (New York: Columbia University Press, 1982), pp. 77 and 235–36, n. 107.

29. This poster is discussed by V. S. Naipaul in *Among the Believers* (New York: Knopf, 1981), pp. 24–25. He understands it as an allegory of blood and revenge in which Khomeini is saved and avenged but in which only Khomeini has a personality, the woman's back being toward the viewer. (I thank Barry Rosen for this reference.)

30. Artist: Hasan Esma'ilzada.

31. Michael Fischer, *Iran: From Religious Dispute to Revolution* (Cambridge, Mass.: Harvard University Press, 1980), p. 182.

PART II

Iran and the Balance of Power in the Middle East

WILLIAM B. QUANDT

Saudi Views of the
Iranian Revolution

When the Iranian revolution began to gather momentum in 1978, few countries were more concerned than the Kingdom of Saudi Arabia. For the Saudi regime, Iran was an important—and troublesome—neighbor. The shah of Iran had viewed his fellow Arab monarchs with barely disguised contempt and had repeatedly made known his intention of dominating the Gulf, which he insisted must always be called the "Persian" Gulf. In addition, he had maintained a strategically important link to Israel, the most tangible element of which was the supply of oil. At the same time, the shah was resolutely pro-Western and shared with Saudi Arabia a strong aversion to radical, potentially destabilizing political movements in the Middle East.

The shah's downfall came at a particularly bad time from the Saudi point of view. Only a few weeks earlier, Egypt's President Anwar Sadat, another pro-Western leader who shared the Saudi aversion to the Soviets and their friends, had concluded an agreement with Israel at Camp David that was soundly denounced in the Arab world. The Saudis, despite pressure from Washington to support the Camp David Accords, had aligned themselves with the Arab consensus at a summit meeting in Baghdad. Diplomatic relations with Egypt were suspended, and the formerly close ties between the two countries were mostly disrupted. Thus, by February 1979, the Saudis could no longer count on Egypt or Iran to help ward off the many threats to stability that afflicted the region.

In this troubled atmosphere, what worried the Saudis most about the Iranian revolution was not the personal fate of the shah, but the specter of a mass-based revolution bringing about the downfall of a conservative monarchy. If this were to prove contagious in the Middle East, many of the Arab Gulf states, as well as countries such as Jordan, Morocco, and of course Saudi Arabia, could be vulnerable to the same type of upheaval.

For the Saudis, it was a source of particular embarrassment that the revolution in Iran called itself Islamic. The Saudis, after all, had for many years sought to portray themselves as the leaders of an Islamic grouping of nations. They could point to their own close ties to Islam, dating from the original compact between the founder of the Saud dynasty and Imam Mohammad b. 'Abd al-Vahhab in the mid-eighteenth century. In an earlier era, the so-called Wahabi movement could even have been seen as a revolutionary Islamic force in its own right, but since the 1930s it had served predominantly to help legitimize the Saud family's claim to rule in the Arabian Peninsula and to enforce a strict social and religious code on a somewhat diverse and dispersed population. Thus the Khomeini revolution in Iran was seen as an ideological threat to Saudi Arabia as well as a change in the strategic situation.

Threats to the Balance of Power

As a comparatively conservative regime with a general preference for preserving the status quo, Saudi Arabia saw the upheaval in Iran as a serious threat to the existing balance of power. On the positive side, the chaos within Iran might temporarily weaken Iran's ability to cause trouble elsewhere in the Middle East, and this the Saudis might welcome. At the same time, a weak Iran might tempt Soviet intervention, and this ultimately could prove to be a very serious threat to the Saudi regime. In addition, a weak Iran would mean that Iraq could play a more assertive role in the region, and that too could have ambivalent consequences for Saudi Arabia.

All of these concerns meant that the initial Saudi reaction to the advent of a new political order in Iran in early 1979 was one of caution. Despite the shrill attacks emanating from Tehran against Saudi Arabia and other conservative Arab monarchies, the Saudi response was on the whole restrained. There was no attempt to answer Iranian propaganda in kind, and the Saudis seemed to take the attitude that it would be best to allow the Iranian revolution to let off steam and not to try to confront it directly in its early phases. For example, Crown Prince Fahd told an interviewer in January 1980, "We have no problems with Iran at present. We are completely satisfied in this respect, contrary to what prevailed during the shah's regime. Regardless of the statements made now and then by irresponsible persons or organizations abusing and attacking the Kingdom, discussions are under way at a very high level with Iranian officials to unify our voice."[1]

What Fahd must have had in mind when referring to "irresponsible persons attacking the Kingdom" could be seen in a March 1980 broadcast in Arabic from Tehran:

The Saudi authorities are playing the same treacherous role that the deposed shah played in Iran. This role grew in the wake of the shah's departure. The people's funds are being spent on weapons that the people can do without and that are stockpiled in arsenals, not to mention the experts and other services required for this purpose. We do not know against whom these weapons will be used. Will they be used to violate the sanctity of the Al-Haram mosque, to kill the faithful who are there, or to tear apart the bodies of the sons of the people who demonstrate against U.S. imperialism in the streets of Qatif, Safva Saiha, Mobarraz, Hofuf, and Jobayl? These are some of the ways in which the funds of the Muslim people in the Arabian Peninsula are being squandered.[2]

A few days later, another broadcast in Arabic from Tehran was made in the name of the Islamic Revolution Organization in the Arabian Peninsula enjoining the "heroic people of Qatif and Ahsa" (Shi'ite areas) to "challenge the authorities' forces by directing blows at them. Where are the arms which you have bought with our funds and used during the 'Moharram' upheaval? Where are the Molotov cocktails which were so well prepared even by women and children? Where are the iron bars, staves, and stones with which you frightened the authorities' forces and inflicted heavy losses on them during the Holy Mosque upheaval?"[3]

The Oil Shock of 1979

One of the tangible manifestations of the Saudi desire for accommodation rather than confrontation with Iran came in the second quarter of 1979. Iran was vociferously denouncing Saudi Arabia for its oil policy, charging that Saudi overproduction was depriving Iran of the opportunity to return to its natural place in the international oil market. In part as an attempt to deflect this criticism, Saudi Arabia reduced its oil production in April 1979 by 1 million barrels per day, thereby making room for increased Iranian production.[4]

One of the consequences of this move, perhaps unintended, was to send the price of oil on the spot market skyrocketing, so that by year's end the spot price for Saudi crude oil had reached $40 and the official contract price stood at $24, nearly double the price at the beginning of the year. One of the great beneficiaries of this increase in oil prices, of course, was Iran. With less than half the oil production that Iran had maintained during the shah's regime, Khomeini's revolutionary Iran was able to earn more income. In brief, Saudi Arabia and Iran together helped produce the oil crisis of 1979, which had the short-run effect of increasing revenues for both countries but planted seeds for the weakening of OPEC several years later and opened the way for intensified long-term competition between these two major Gulf oil producers.

The Ideological Challenge

Among the most difficult challenges posed by the Iranian revolution for the Kingdom of Saudi Arabia was the ideological attack that was daily launched against the Saudi regime from Tehran. Khomeini in his early writings had been reluctant to draw the conclusion that Islam and monarchy were incompatible, but once he did begin to propound this theme he pursued it relentlessly. Iranian propaganda after Khomeini's assumption of power in February 1979 repeated this point, calling on the Arabs across the Gulf to rise up against their corrupt hereditary leaders. It was not only Khomeini's insistence on the incompatibility of Islam and monarchical rule that worried the Saudi regime. It was also the Iranian model of mass mobilization in the name of Islam. Nothing in recent Saudi political experience was comparable to the Iranian revolution, and the whole political culture of the Kingdom was aimed at avoiding any such politicization of the population. Islam was extremely important in Saudi Arabia, but as a conservative and legitimizing force, not as a source of revolutionary transformation.

The other theme in Iranian propaganda under Khomeini that disquieted the Saudi regime was the strident anti-American tone and the strong call for nonalignment. Even before the Iranian revolution, the Saudis had been sensitive to the charge that they were too closely tied to the United States, and now that Khomeini was repeating this accusation the Saudis felt even more on the defensive. Thus, the ideological challenge from Iran took two forms: that of attacking the Saudi regime as incompatible with true Islam and that of accusing the Saudis of being a forward base of American imperialism in the Middle East.

Iranian Subversion

Evidence of Iran's intention to destabilize its Arab neighbors was not long in coming. At the time of the Mecca mosque affair in November 1979, the Iranians were quick to call for the overthrow of the Saud dynasty in the name of Islam. Many Saudis initially believed that Iran was behind the seizure of the mosque. (In fact, the Mecca insurgents had nothing to do with Iran and were anti-Shi'i in their propaganda.) Shortly thereafter, Shi'is in Saudi Arabia's eastern province carried out violent demonstrations, encouraged and perhaps inspired by the Khomeini example.

Saudi security authorities began to watch carefully for evidence of Iranian subversion. Iranian pilgrims making the *hajj* were subjected to careful scrutiny and were not allowed to carry out political activity. This became an annual preoccupation for the Saudis, and there were occasional clashes between pro-Khomeini zealots and Saudi security forces in Mecca.

The most tangible evidence of Iran's attempts to export revolution to the Arab side of the Gulf came in December 1981, when Bahraini authorities announced the arrest of some sixty Arab conspirators who had received training in sabotage techniques at a center near Isfahan. Several Saudis were among those arrested. While little information was made public about the plans of those who were arrested, it appears as if a coup was envisaged, and some reports maintained that the Iranian navy was prepared to intervene in support once the conspirators had made their move. In the end, the plot was unraveled early on, but it nonetheless caused a tremor of concern throughout the Gulf. Within weeks, Saudi Arabia and Bahrain announced that they had signed a security pact.

The Iran-Iraq War

Just as the success of the Iranian revolution in February 1979 had caused considerable ambivalence among Saudi officials, so also the outbreak of war between Iran and Iraq in September 1980 carried a mixed message. On the one hand, there were many Saudis who hoped to see Khomeini's regime toppled, and if the Iraqis could do this quickly and efficiently, so much the better. On the other hand, Saudi Arabia had little interest in seeing Iraq emerge as a victorious military power in the Gulf. Thus, the Saudis witnessed the outbreak of war with apprehension and a direct concern that the violence might spread beyond Iran and Iraq. This fear was justified to some extent, and during the first anxious weeks of the war the possibility that Iraq would seek to use the territory of other Gulf states to launch attacks against Iran was taken seriously. It was only with some diplomatic effort that a broadening of the war was prevented.

Shortly after the fighting began in late September 1980, Baghdad announced that "King Khalid affirmed the support of the Kingdom of Saudi Arabia for Iraq in its pan-Arab battle and conflict with the Persians, the enemies of the Arab nation." With uncharacteristic speed, a mere six hours later, Riyadh was putting out its own version of the Khalid-Saddam Hosain exchange, noting that the king had "expressed his interest and his good fraternal feelings" to Saddam, confirmed the "depth of the fraternal relations between the two sister countries," and asked God to "guide our steps in the interest of our Arab and Islamic nations."[5] Clearly, the Saudis were not about to be stampeded into a confrontational public position toward Iran. Whatever their private sentiments may have been, discretion marked their official statements at the outset of the war and continued to do so in succeeding months.

One of the early Saudi reactions to the outbreak of fighting was to request that the United States help augment Saudi Arabia's air defense capabilities by sending four Airborne Warning and Control Systems (AWACS) aircraft to Saudi Arabia to fly patrols that would allow the early detection of any Iranian aircraft intruding into Saudi air space. In addition, the United States provided assistance to Saudi Arabia in the form of naval patrols in the region. More extreme developments, however, such as building U.S. air bases in the Arabian Peninsula to provide for regional defense, were hardly more welcome in the new atmosphere than they had been previously.

As the war between Iran and Iraq dragged on, Saudi Arabia increasingly committed itself to the Iraqi side of the conflict. The most tangible form of assistance was financial, and from September 1980 until the spring of 1982 the Saudis provided economic assistance to Iraq at the rate of as much as $1 billion per month. Theoretically, this assistance took the form of loans to be repaid after Iraq had recovered its capacity to export oil. By mid-1982, however, Saudi Arabia was beginning to tire of the game of helping Iraq, and reports began to spread that the Saudis were cutting back on aid. This coincided, perhaps not by chance, with a reversal of Iraq's fortunes on the battlefield and the reemergence of Iran as the dominant military power in the area. Increasingly, one began to sense that Saudi Arabia was hedging its bets.

By mid-1983, Saudi "nonalignment" in the Iran-Iraq dispute may have been further encouraged by some signs of moderation in Iran, coupled with the decimation of the pro-Soviet Tuda party. At the same time, Soviet supplies of arms to Iraq were resumed, helping to insure a stalemate on the battlefield but also bringing the specter of a return of Soviet influence to Iraq after years of cool relations between Moscow and Baghdad. In such circumstances, the Saudis seemed to move toward neutrality, while discreetly urging an end to the war.

From the narrow perspective of oil politics, one could argue that the Iran-Iraq War was beneficial to Saudi Arabia. After all, without the war another 2 to 3 million barrels per day of oil would probably be thrown onto the international market. This would result in a further softening of prices, unless, of course, Saudi Arabia were prepared to make further deep cuts in production.

While the Saudis were clearly aware that the end of the Iran-Iraq War would present them with new challenges in the oil market, they nonetheless appeared to favor a truce. As long as the war dragged on, the Iraqis would make heavy financial claims on the Saudis and other Gulf oil-producing states. In addition, there would always be the chance that Iraq might deliver an effective blow to the Iranian oil terminals on Kharg Island, to which Iran might respond by threatening to attack the Saudi terminals at Ras Tannura or to close the Strait of Hormuz, thereby blocking most Saudi exports.

During 1983, the danger of an escalation in the Iran-Iraq War became a preoccupation for the Saudis. The Iraqis were under severe economic pressure, and the Saudis certainly did not want to see the regime collapse. They thus favored the French decision to sell it Super Etendard aircraft with the capability of launching Exocet missiles. At a minimum, this might provide the Iraqis with a deterrent against further massive Iranian attacks, but the Saudis did not want to see the Exocets used in ways that might provoke Iranian retaliation. Therefore, they reportedly urged the Iraqis not to attack Kharg Island or international shipping. Iraqi rhetoric suggested that they paid little attention to the Saudi warnings.

Adding to Saudi reasons for seeking an end to the Iran-Iraq War has been the debilitating impact of that dispute on inter-Arab relations. Syria and Libya have aligned themselves with Iran, and Syria in particular has seemed determined to help bring down the regime of Saddam Hosain. As usual, the Saudis have disliked taking sides in such a dispute. They may hope that, with the end of the Iran-Iraq War, inter-Arab relations will become less fractious.

For reasons of Arab politics, as well as those involving oil, Gulf stability, and security, the Saudis appear to have concluded that the Iran-Iraq War is a threat that must be brought to an end, but apart from offering some financial assistance as part of a postwar "reconstruction fund" (i.e., the reparations demanded by Iran) they have done little to help mediate the dispute. Like many others, they may well believe that the war will not end until either Khomeini or Saddam Hosain has passed from the scene.

The Gulf Cooperation Council

With the outbreak of the Iran-Iraq War, the periodic consultations among the leaders of the Arab Gulf states and Saudi Arabia were viewed as insufficient, and in May 1981 the Gulf Cooperation Council was formally created, with Saudi Arabia assuming the role of senior partner. Iraq was not invited to participate, a development which would have been less likely in the absence of the war. Some observers expected great things from the Gulf Cooperation Council—in the economic field, in the security field, and in areas of political and cultural exchange—but the results in the first years were somewhat mixed. It met with regularity but did not succeed in developing common positions on most controversial issues, nor did it go very far in developing programs for joint security planning.

One of the difficult tests for the Saudis, and for the other members of the GCC, came from the reassertion of Iranian power as the revolution was consolidated and as Iran regained strength on the battlefield. The reactions to this development in the Gulf were not uniform. The United Arab Emirates took the lead in adopting an accommodating posture toward Iran. Others were reluctant to seek dialogue with Iran. The Saudis, as usual, held the decisive edge in this debate between those who saw wisdom in accommodating Iran and those who considered Iran a serious danger to the conservative regimes of the Peninsula that must be resisted by all means. As time passed, the Saudis seemed to be inclined to follow the Emirates' line of avoiding actions that might antagonize Iran.

OPEC Politics

In addition to the ideological and military challenges arising from the revolution, the Saudis were confronted with competition from Iran in the oil market. By 1981 Iran was beginning to seek a return to normal in its oil production and marketing. While the Islamic regime in Tehran was unable to bring oil production back up to the high levels of the shah's era, it was capable of producing between 2.5 and 3 million barrels per day. However, world demand for oil was rapidly declining by the time Iran sought to reenter the market, and in order to attract customers the Iranians were obliged to discount their oil by a substantial amount. This set the stage for severe competition between Iran, which was violating OPEC practices, and Saudi Arabia, which was attempting to preserve the OPEC price of $34 per barrel in a shrinking market. To do this, the Saudis were obliged to cut their production substantially, and they found it annoying, to say the least, that Iran was expanding output at the same time.

In OPEC meetings beginning with the spring 1982 session, Iran launched sharp attacks on Saudi production policy, arguing that Saudi Arabia had no right to such a large share of the oil market. With a small population, Saudi Arabia should make do with a modest share of the market, allowing the larger countries, such as Iran, Nigeria, Venezuela, and Indonesia, to produce at their maximum capacity to meet their revenue requirements. The Iranian argument met with considerable sympathy, and the Saudis found themselves under unprecedented pressure within OPEC to play the part of swing producer in a declining market, that is to say, to make the essential production cuts necessary to defend the $34 price.

By late 1982, it was becoming increasingly clear that the $34 price could not be maintained unless Saudi Arabia were prepared to reduce production to intolerably low levels. When the OPEC ministers met in January 1983, the question of price reductions, accompanied by a formula for allocating market shares, arose for the first time. The Iranians argued successfully that their share of the OPEC market should be increased to the point where Iran could count on marketing nearly all of the oil that it was capable of producing—about 2.5 million barrels per day. According to the same formula, Saudi production would be held at less than half of productive capacity—around 4 to 5 million barrels per day. For reasons that remain somewhat unclear, the Saudis engineered a breakdown of the January 1983 OPEC meeting over the ostensible issue of price differentials between grades of crude oil. Nonetheless, before long the OPEC ministers reconvened in London, and in March they announced a formal reduction of the market price from $34 to $29 per barrel and a market-sharing agreement that essentially reflected the Iranian point of view.

This willingness of most members of OPEC, including the Saudis, to accommodate Iran's demands suggested that Iran's power was on the upswing. The agreement reached in London will be subject to strain unless there is a recovery in the demand for OPEC oil. With demand hovering around 18 million barrels per day, Saudi Arabia was able to accept that its production would be near 5 million barrels per day, and a surprisingly smooth adjustment was made in the 1983-84 budget to reflect the lower revenues. Throughout 1984-85, there seems little likelihood that either Saudi Arabia or Iran will be able to increase output significantly. This is probably a tolerable situation, but two types of problems could arise: if the Iran-Iraq War intensifies and Iranian production is hit, then Saudi Arabia might seek to increase its market share, which could provoke a sharp Iranian reaction; alternatively, an increase in demand to 20 million barrels per day might lead the Saudis to argue that they should get the bulk of the increase as the swing producer. This latter argument would find little support in OPEC, and Iran could be expected to lead the campaign against a larger Saudi market share.

This analysis suggests that Saudi Arabia and Iran will remain economic competitors as well as political and military rivals. In these circumstances, the Saudis will be influenced by Iran's position of power, and it seems unlikely that considerations of economic advantage will tempt the Saudis to confront the more powerful regime in Tehran. If Saudi Arabia and Iran can contain their disputes, and if the Saudis are willing to keep oil production at comparatively low levels, Iran will gain economically, while the Saudis may hope that their potentially troublesome neighbor will leave them in peace. For the world, this would mean high but stable oil prices. All-out economic competition between Tehran and Riyadh, in contrast, could bring a price collapse, whereas military confrontation could produce price increases. In brief, the price of oil in the 1980s will be heavily influenced by the course of Iranian-Saudi relations. If the Saudis remain true to form, they will not be the ones seeking confrontation.

Conclusions

By mid-1983, the Saudi posture of avoiding confrontation with Iran appeared to be paying off. Rather than moving into the Soviet sphere of influence, Iran had instead cracked down on leftist elements, and Soviet-Iranian relations were subject to serious strains. In addition, the government in Tehran began to adopt a somewhat more accommodating tone toward the Gulf Cooperation Council and even received a GCC mediator seeking an end to the Iran-Iraq War.

Along with these encouraging signs, the Saudis can take some satisfaction in the fact that Iran has not been able to export its revolution— although not for lack of trying. The war with Iraq has apparently reached a tenuous stalemate, and the prospect of a decisive Iranian victory has faded, although a widening of the war if Iraq should lash out in desperation cannot be precluded. There have been no further occurrences of attempts at subversion such as the Bahrain affair, and even the potentially divisive issues of oil production and pricing have been skillfully managed, at least temporarily.

Saudis may well therefore conclude that Iran is entering a somewhat less violent and radical phase of its revolution. If so, Saudi Arabia will still face problems in its relations with Iran as a powerful neighbor and as a competitor within OPEC. But Saudis are familiar with the imperatives of state-to-state balance-of-power politics. They play this game with some skill. It is "Iran the revolution," not "Iran the state," that has been the source of greatest concern to the rulers in Riyadh, and as Iran begins to behave more as a normal player in the somewhat chaotic Middle East game, the Saudis will breathe a bit more easily.

Notes

1. *Al-Safir* (Beirut), January 9, 1980.
2. BBC monitoring service, March 11, 1980.
3. BBC monitoring service, March 17, 1980.
4. William B. Quandt, *Saudi Arabia's Oil Policy* (Washington, D.C.: Brookings Institution, 1982), pp. 15–21.
5. Baghdad, Iraqi News Agency, September 15, 1980; Riyadh, Saudi Press Agency, September 25, 1980.

JIMAN TAGAVI

The Iran-Iraq War:
The First Three Years

The war between Iran and Iraq has been a puzzle to most observers.
Expected by the Iraqis to be another "seven-day war," this fratricidal
conflict has raged on for over three years at a cost of over a hundred
thousand dead, over a quarter-million wounded, and billions of dollars
in military expenditures and in property damage to both sides. This
paper examines the causes and conduct of the war, its effects on the
internal politics of Iran and on regional political alignments, and its
consequences for the economies of the two countries and then offers
some ideas about its future course. I shall begin by briefly highlighting
some of the more important events in the relationship between the two
countries in the twenty-five years preceding the outbreak of the war.[1]

Events Leading to the War

In 1955 both countries participated in the signing of the Baghdad
Pact, the purpose of which was to curb Soviet influence in the area.
With the overthrow of the Iraqi monarchy by the national forces led
by General Qasem in 1958, relations between Iran and Iraq cooled
considerably. The subsequent decade witnessed a total of five governments
and three coups d'etat in Iraq. A period of stability was inaugurated
by the ascendancy of the Ba'th party in 1968. Relations between Iran
and Iraq worsened with the Ba'th's rise to power, and in 1969 the shah
abrogated the Frontier Treaty of 1937, which had placed the border
between Iran and Iraq on the Iranian side of the Shatt al-Arab except
for the four miles opposite the island of Abadan. When the British
withdrew from the Gulf in 1971, the shah took over the islands of Abu
Musa, Greater Tunb, and Lesser Tunb, at the entrance to the Strait of
Hormuz, further straining relations between the two countries. Moreover,
since 1969 he had been providing arms to the Kurdish rebels in Iraq.
The hostile relations between the two countries came to an end,
however, with the Algiers Accord of 1975. Under the terms of the accord,

(1) Iran was to stop all aid to the Kurdish rebels; (2) the two countries were to discontinue their propaganda war and to cease interfering in each other's internal affairs, and Iraq was to abandon its opposition to the Iranian occupation of Abu Musa, Greater Tunb, and Lesser Tunb; and (3) the border between the two states was to be the middle of the Shatt al-Arab.[2] When in September 1978 the shah, faced with internal opposition from religiously inspired demonstrators, asked for the expulsion of Khomeini from Iraq, Saddam Hosain complied.

The Ba'th regime initially welcomed the shah's fall in January 1979 because of his heavy-handed manipulation of regional politics and his self-designation as "policeman of the Gulf." However, as early as April Iraqi apprehensions about the new Iranian regime were being expressed by Shebli al-Aisani, a top Ba'th official: "While talking of Islam they spread chauvinist, anti-Arab ideas, and they have reasserted their claim to the three Gulf islands and Bahrain."[3]

During the summer of 1979, Saddam Hosain took over the presidency from Hasan al-Bakr and initiated a purge of the Revolutionary Command Council, some of whose members were unhappy with his monopolization of power.[4] Some of those purged were Shi'is whom Saddam had accused of complicity with the Syrians in planning his ouster. As a result, the relationship between Iraq and Syria—one that had been cordial since Egypt's decision to sign the Camp David Accords with Israel in 1978, at the expense of the other Arab participants in the conflict—disintegrated.

Meanwhile, Shi'i demonstrations in Bahrain, Kuwait, Saudi Arabia, and Iraq indicated to the ruling circles of the Gulf their vulnerability in the face of Iran's call for the Islamization of their regimes. Michael Hudson had written in 1977 that "the central problem of government in the Arab world is political legitimacy" and that Islam was no longer capable of providing it.[5] Contrary to Hudson, Islam was still an important source of legitimacy for the Gulf monarchies. However, Saddam Hosain's secularist Ba'th party had completely abandoned Islam as a source of legitimacy, and Saddam felt particularly vulnerable to Shi'i propaganda against him. The fact that he was Sunni and the majority (55 percent) of Iraqis were Shi'i exacerbated his problems. Furthermore, the Iraqi Shi'i Da'va and Mojahedin were resorting to guerrilla activities against the regime in the aftermath of the Iranian revolution, thus bringing to the surface the Ba'th's sectarian problems.[6] By October 1979 Saddam was threatening to use his forces against anyone who interfered in the affairs of the Gulf states. Iran was, of course, the object of his warning. Iraqi officials now began demanding the return of the islands of Abu Musa, Greater Tunb, and Lesser Tunb, the renegotiation of the Algiers Accord, and better treatment for the Arab minority in Khuzestan. The clerical forces in Tehran responded by instigating attacks by the Revolutionary Guards against the Iraqi embassy in Tehran and the Iraqi consulates in Kermanshah and Khorramshahr.[7]

The downfall of the liberals in the aftermath of the takeover of the American embassy in Tehran in November 1979 and the assumption of control of the Majlis by the Islamic Republican Party in the general elections in early 1980 convinced the Ba'th leadership that the clerical forces in Iran were in control and would persist in attempting to export their revolution. Hostilities between the two countries became progressively overt, with many border incidents, during the first half of 1980. Because of Iran's instability at this time, the Iraqis enjoyed more opportunities for disruption, including sabotage of the Iranian oil installations and material aid to the Kurdish rebels in Iran. Two attempted military coups in Iran had come to nothing, thereby eliminating the Iraqis' hopes for an internal Iranian solution to their problems. By the summer of 1980 the Ba'th leadership in Baghdad had decided on an invasion of Iran. Saddam had received the acquiescence, if not the blessing, of Jordan and the Gulf states, including Saudi Arabia, which he had visited in August before embarking on his venture.[8]

The War and Internal Iranian Politics

Iraq and Iran had been involved in the intermittent shelling of each other's border towns and villages since the end of August, and on September 19 Iraq seized territory around Zain al-Qaus and Saif Sa'ad that was to have been returned to it in compliance with the Algiers Accord.[9] On September 17 Saddam abrogated the accord, and within a few days the Iraqi armed forces had invaded Iran from three major areas.[10] In four days they were within 15–20 kilometers of the major Iranian cities of Khorramshahr, Ahvaz, and Dezful. The quick victory envisioned by Saddam Hosain did not materialize, however, and in mid-November the Iraqis' advance came to a halt.[11] They had succeeded in capturing three chunks of Iranian territory: a strip opposite the Iraqi city of Solaimaniyya in the north, a second strip running from Qasr-e Shirin to Mehran, across from Baghdad, and a much larger area extending from Dezful to Abadan (see Map 1). The heavy casualties sustained by the Iraqis in their capture of Khorramshahr from the determined Iranian revolutionary guards dissuaded them from attempting the capture of Dezful, Ahvaz, and Abadan, and from mid-November until the following May both sides were content to maintain their positions while engaging in constant artillery duels.

Why had Saddam Hosain so miscalculated the Iranians' ability and determination to resist him? First, he had believed that the Iranian armed forces had disintegrated in the first year and a half of the revolution

IRANIAN TERRITORY CAPTURED BY IRAQ   Map 1
(Winter, 1980)

LEGEND

━━━ • ━━━   INTERNATIONAL BOUNDARY

━ • ━ • ━   PROVINCE BOUNDARY

▒▒▒▒   IRAQI OCCUPIED TERRITORY

because of the purges they had been subjected to by the clerical forces, fearful of a military coup. However, while many of the top officers had been executed and others had been retired, the armed forces still had a large sector of junior officers and about a hundred thousand men. Furthermore, a large number of citizens had received military training through the shah's compulsory military service program. More importantly, the shah's large stockpiles of weapons and ammunition were mostly intact, although there were shortages of spare parts, mainly for aircraft.[12] The Revolutionary Guards, which had developed out of the militia units formed around the various neighborhood committees that controlled the urban areas after the fall of Bakhtiar, proved through their faith and determination to be outstanding fighters against whom the Iraqi regulars were at a distinct disadvantage.[13] Their willingness to become martyrs eliminated frontal attacks and hand-to-hand combat as options for the Iraqis, especially after the battle of Khorramshahr.

The Iraqis had also believed that the various ethnic groups who were dissatisfied with the clerically dominated Tehran regime—the Khuzestan Arabs, the Baluchis, the Azerbaijanis—and the young guerrilla groups, the Mojahedin and the Feda'iyyin, which had been instrumental in the fall of Bakhtiar but were now being harshly treated, would take advantage of the opportunity to overthrow it. Furthermore, Bakhtiar and Ovaisi, who had been in Iraq most of the summer, had convinced the Iraqis that there was also a strong royalist and nationalist stratum in Iran, especially in the armed forces, that would use the occasion to seize power. That it did not is an indication of either its paucity in numbers or its recognition of the strength of the revolutionary forces in Iran.[14] The decision of the ethnic minorities (except the Kurds) and the Feda'iyyin and Mojahedin to support the central government's effort against Iraq was an indication of that strength and a reaffirmation of the fact that crises, especially war, commonly evoke cooperation among groups otherwise in opposition to the ruling government.

If Saddam Hosain had hoped by his invasion of Iran to eliminate or silence the clerical forces that were agitating against him and the other Gulf leaders, he accomplished the exact opposite. These forces, which had been engaged in a bitter struggle against liberal and radical elements since the fall of Bakhtiar, had earlier received a new lease on life from their supporters' takeover of the American embassy. That incident allowed the clerical forces of the IRP to use the wealth of information captured in the embassy to discredit many of the liberals for their contacts with the Americans while discreetly keeping silent on such contacts on the part of IRP clerics (e.g., Beheshti).[15] Furthermore, the "Followers of the Line of the Imam," under clerical supervision, became the most vocal anti-American group in Iran. The youth-oriented Feda'iyyin, Mojahedin, and Paikar groups had no choice but to support the takeover of the embassy; however, now their struggles against the clerical forces were being explained by the IRP as an indication of their complicity with the Americans. The IRP clerics' refusal to release the hostages was directly linked to their appreciation of the hostage crisis as helping them to consolidate their political position at the expense of liberals such as Bazargan, Qotbzada, Bani-Sadr, and the various leftist groups.

The outbreak of the war and the advance of the Iraqi forces into Iran gave the clerical forces another opportunity to undermine their liberal and radical opposition. Bani-Sadr, who had become president as a result of the last-minute withdrawal of the IRP front-runner Jalal Farsi, was confronted by an IRP-controlled Majlis that sought to undermine him by portraying his post as purely ceremonial. In the battle between the clerically dominated IRP and Bani-Sadr and the liberals, Bani-Sadr was often on the losing side.[16] His candidates for various posts were rejected, while the IRP imposed many of its candidates upon him.

The start of the war gave Bani-Sadr the opportunity to take center stage because of his presidential role as the commander of the armed forces. He repeatedly toured the war front, assuring himself of media coverage that he hoped would increase his popularity and strengthen his hand in his dealings with the IRP. The IRP, of course, was quick to respond through its members on the Supreme Defense Council. As Bani-Sadr sought to strengthen the role of the armed forces, his clerical opponents in the IRP-dominated council, concerned about giving too much power to a military that they suspected of monarchist sympathies, advocated strict control over them, especially through the use of the Revolutionary Guards. While Bani-Sadr's position as the commander of the armed forces was being undermined by the clerics, he was repeatedly criticized by the IRP for Iran's initial poor showing in the war.

The IRP also utilized the war to alienate the two most important guerrilla groups, the Feda'iyyin and Mojahedin. The two groups had made a valiant effort in the defense of Khorramshahr at the beginning of the war, and the IRP, concerned that this would enhance their popularity, ordered their removal from Khorramshahr. Assigning the role of defending the revolution to itself alone, the IRP portrayed its various opponents as un-Islamic and as collaborators inspired by the forces of imperialism. It is noteworthy that the Mojahedin had become the largest guerrilla-based political organization in Iran mainly because it shared with the IRP the umbrella of Islamic legitimacy. The Feda'iyyin, which had no recourse to such legitimization, was unable to expand its membership as much. Both groups, however, were charged with being misguided and un-Islamic because of their opposition to the authoritarian conduct of the IRP.[17]

During the spring of 1981 a de facto alliance developed between the Mojahedin and Bani-Sadr, both locked in conflict with the IRP. Bani-Sadr's long-promised Iranian counteroffensive finally took place in May 1981, though the results were not very impressive. When, in March of that year, Bani-Sadr ordered his supporters to detain and disarm the Hezbollahis (IRP toughs) who were disrupting a rally of his supporters in Tehran, the IRP leadership accused the president of taking the law into his own hands and called for his prosecution. Bani-Sadr and his aides went into hiding and eventually escaped to France.[18] The Mojahedin came out in support of Bani-Sadr, and fighting ensued between it and the Revolutionary Guards, forcing the former to go underground. The IRP party headquarters was bombed (apparently by Mojahedin supporters), killing over seventy top party leaders including Ayatollah Beheshti.[19]

With the suppression of Bani-Sadr, his liberal supporters, the Mojahedin, and the minority-faction Feda'iyyin guerrillas, the IRP leadership continued the counteroffensive against the Iraqi forces, and, in September 1981, one year after the start of the war, the Iranian military regained full control of Abadan (see Map 2, **A**). This signaled a change of fortunes for the Iranians. On November 29, Bostan, north of Susangerd, was recaptured; consequently, the Iranians were able to regain some seventy towns and villages in the area (see Map 2, **B**).[20] As in the previous year, no major battles took place between December and May.

On May 22, 1982, the Iranians commenced Operation Fath, destroying the Iraqi Fourth Army Corps, which was surrounding Dezful, and pushing the Iraqis back 30–40 kilometers to within 10 kilometers of the border. The Iranians regained 772 square kilometers of territory, inflicting heavy losses of life and equipment on the Iraqis (see Map 2, **C**).[21] Additionally, many Iraqi prisoners were taken. On May 24 the Iranians recaptured Khorramshahr, which they had designated "Khuninshahr," or "City of Blood," during its occupation by the Iraqis. The push for Khorramshahr had begun on April 30 when the Iranians moved down from Ahvaz, forcing about thirty thousand Iraqi soldiers to retreat to Khorramshahr (see Map 2, **D**). With the retreat of the Iraqi army from Khorramshahr, Saddam Hosain announced that he would withdraw his forces from Iranian territory by June 30, 1982, thereby terminating all hostilities.[22]

While Iraq sought to end the conflict at this point, Iran decided to carry the fighting onto Iraqi soil, and on July 13 Iranian forces began a drive toward the city of Basra.[23] The Iraqis put up stiff resistance, and the Iranians were forced to retreat. The Iranians made two other large-scale invasion attempts in 1982, both of which were repulsed by the Iraqis. On October 1, Iranian forces attacked across the border from

IRANIAN VICTORIES

Map 2

(Sept. 1981 – May. 1982)

LEGEND

—·—·—·—	INTERNATIONAL BOUNDARY
—··—··—	PROVINCE BOUNDARY
— — — —	FRONT LINE – APRIL 1. 1982 (APPROX.)
··············	FRONT LINE – NOVEMBER 1980 (APPROX.)

⟡

A   CAPTURE OF ABADAN
B   CAPTURE OF BOSTAN AREA
C   MAY ADVANCES AROUND DEZFUL
D   MAY ADVANCES AROUND KHORRAMSHAHR

0   50   100   150
Kilometers

Mehran

Tigris

I R A N

C

Dezful   *Karun*

al-
Amara   B
Bostan
Susangerd   K H U Z E S T A N
Hamidiyya

I R A Q

Hovaiza   Ahvaz

al-
Naseriyya

D

Khorramshahr

Basra

Shatt al-Arab   Abadan
Omm Qasr   A

KUWAIT   P e r s i a n
G u l f

i.e. romann

Baghdad.[24] Although they gained some territory, they were unable to break through toward Baghdad. On November 1 the Iranians started another large-scale invasion, this time across from Dezful, and, although successful in gaining some territory, were stopped by Iraqis.[25]

On February 16, 1983, Iran initiated a new offensive in the Fagih area of Misra Province; however, they were again repulsed (see Map 3, **A**).[26] On March 3, Iraqi planes attacked the Nauruz oil fields, northwest of Kharg Island, damaging three Iranian oil wells and causing the biggest marine oil spill in history.[27] In early April it seemed that the Gulf states might succeed in bringing about a cease-fire between Iran and Iraq that would allow the wells to be capped, thus stopping the increasing damage to Gulf marine life and, more importantly, serving as a first step toward a resolution of the conflict. However, just when it seemed a compromise had been arranged, on April 13, Iran began another offensive on an 11-kilometer front west of Dezful, which Iraq was able to contain.[28]

Iran's next offensive began on July 21 in the far north across from the Iranian town of Piranshahr, followed by another offensive on July 30 across from Mehran (see Map 3, **B** and **C**).[29] These last two offensives were limited in scope, and the Iranians were able to achieve their objectives—the control of small but important pockets of territory.

In October 1983, the Iranians captured Panjvin, which is about 16 kilometers inside Iraq across from the Iranian town of Marivan (see Map 3, **D**).[30] Panjvin is 145 kilometers east of Kirkuk, the only oil field from which Iraq is currently exporting oil. Should the Iranians penetrate to Kirkuk and stop Iraq's oil exports, Baghdad's ability to continue the war will be greatly hampered and it will be only a matter of time before the Iraqi regime falls.

Realignment in Regional Politics

From the inception of the war, Saddam has depicted it as an ethnic conflict between Persians and Arabs and accused Khomeini of being a turbaned shah seeking to continue the shah's expansionist policies in the region. Khomeini has replied in kind by accusing Saddam of being an Iraqi shah who has forsaken Islam and embraced an alien ideology (Arab socialism) and who rules by means of a SAVAK-type secret police.[31] The Iranian propaganda against the Iraqi regime seems to have worked, judging from the repression of politically active Iraqi Shi'i groups such as the Da'va and the Mojahedin. On the other hand, the Iraqi depiction of the conflict as one between Arabs and Persians lost much of its credibility when Syria, Libya, Algeria, and the People's Democratic Republic of Yemen (PDRY) took Iran's side in the conflict, with Syria being Iran's most important ally.

IRAN – IRAQ WAR
(February – October, 1983)

Map 3

LEGEND

A OFFENSIVE NEAR FAGIH – FEBRUARY

B OFFENSIVE NEAR PIRANSHAHR – JULY 21

C OFFENSIVE NEAR MEHRAN – JULY 30

D CAPTURE OF PANJVIN – OCTOBER

```
0    50   100   150   200
Kilometers
```

The enmity between Syria and Iraq had sprung initially from the divergent ideological views held by the Ba'th leadership of the two countries.[32] The differences between the two regimes were exacerbated by Iraqi criticism of Syria's disengagement agreement with Israel in 1974 and its decision to become protector of the Christian side in the Lebanese civil war in 1975-76. A rapprochement developed between Iraq and Syria when Sadat signed the Camp David Accords. The increasing military presence of Israel in southern Lebanon also caused a lessening of tensions between the two Ba'th regimes. Furthermore, both were alarmed by the resurgence of sectarianism in their countries as a result of the rise of the Islamic opposition movement in Iran during 1978. Saddam and Hafez al-Asad had met in Damascus and worked out the details of a federation between the two states, but the federation idea had collapsed when Saddam took over the presidency and purged the pro-Syrian members of the Revolutionary Command Council. There was a sectarian dimension to the conflict between Saddam and Asad, since a number of the purged Iraqi leaders were Shi'is; Asad and his associates are mostly 'Alavis (a Shi'i sect) in a predominantly Sunni Syria. This sectarian element gained prominence after Khomeini's rise to power in Iran and his forced polarization of the issue of Islam and secularism. Although Khomeini never differentiated between Shi'a and Sunni Islam, his secularist opponents in Iraq, who were mostly Sunni, accused him of heresy and un-Islamic behavior. Ironically, the Muslim Brotherhood in Syria, which is Sunni, seeks to topple Asad precisely because of his secularist ideology and governance.

Syria was joined by Libya in taking Iran's side in the war. Qadhdhafi, who had become isolated in inter-Arab politics by the summer of 1980, proposed a merger with Syria. Although nothing came of the federated state, Syria and Libya were joined in supporting Iran by their allies since 1977 in the Steadfastness Front, Algeria and the PDRY.[33] The Palestine Liberation Organization, which had welcomed the Iranian revolution for its support of its cause, tried initially to act as an arbiter in the conflict, but when Iran reprimanded it for these efforts it became much less vocal about the war.

Saudi Arabia, the Gulf states, and Jordan, Iraq's allies at the beginning of the war, were soon joined by Egypt, which used the war as an opportunity to escape from its isolated position in Arab politics in the aftermath of the Camp David Accords. Sudan followed suit, even sending troops to fight alongside the Iraqis.[34] This pattern of alignments has held throughout the three years of the war; however, since the summer of 1982, when Iran recaptured most of its lost territories, Saudi Arabia and the Gulf states have muted their support of Iraq and cut back on their economic aid to Saddam. Furthermore, Saudi Arabia and the Gulf states are currently (in November 1983) acting as a restraining force on Iraq, which has acquired French Exocet missiles and Super Etendard jets capable of destroying Iran's main oil-loading terminal on Kharg Island. Iraq has been warned by the Gulf and Saudi leaders not to attack Kharg Island, since Iran would then most likely take retaliatory measures against their oil installations and block the Strait of Hormuz, stopping oil exports from the Gulf.

The Effect of the War on the Economies of Iran and Iraq

The war has had a severe negative impact on the economies of Iran and Iraq. The petro-propelled economic development programs of both countries have been greatly hampered, and it will take years after the termination of hostilities for them to regain the development momentum they have lost as a result of the war.

Iraq began the war with a robust and healthy economy, having $35 billion in international reserves and a number of large-scale projects in progress.[35] Ironically, it was the Iranian revolution that had helped Iraq to accrue these reserves. The shutdown of Iranian oil facilities beginning in September 1978 had precipitated a rise in oil prices from $12 a barrel to $24 a barrel by early 1979. Iraq was able to expand its production during the six months in which Iranian facilities were closed as well as receive twice as much for the oil it was marketing.

The three years of the war, however, have imposed great stress on the Iraqi economy. While Iraq was exporting 3.3 million barrels of petroleum a day in September 1980, the closing of the Gulf to Iraqi shipping by the Iranian navy at the start of the war and Syria's decision in April 1982 to close down the pipeline that carries Iraqi oil through Syria to Lebanon have reduced Iraqi oil exports to 650,000 barrels a day.[36] Furthermore, while Iraq received $20–30 billion in aid from the Gulf states and Saudi Arabia in 1982, it was only promised $6 billion by these countries for the first six months of 1983, not all of which, the Iraqis contend, has been forthcoming.[37]

The combination of Arab aid and large international reserves had allowed Saddam to follow a policy of "guns and butter" for the first two and a half years of the war. Most of the development projects that were under way when the war began were pursued by the Iraqi government until the end of 1982. However, the Gulf countries' refusal to maintain the former level of aid to Iraq and the reduction of its international currency and gold reserves to $5–6 billion by early 1983 forced the Ba'th regime to institute an austerity program entailing a 20–25 percent reduction in government spending for 1983.[38] Furthermore, the Iraqis have been forced to defer payments to Japanese, French,

British, and German companies that have been engaged in projects in Iraq and to arrange for loans from international banking consortiums. In March 1983 the United States extended $450 million in credits to Iraq to be used toward the purchase of U.S. agricultural commodities.[39]

The financial woes facing Saddam are ominous. One of the reasons he has not confronted the kind of large-scale domestic uprising many Iranian leaders expected is that most Iraqis have been benefiting economically from the government's domestic development programs and have therefore been willing to support the regime.[40] How long this support will continue now that the regime is unable to provide the same level of economic benefits as before is difficult to predict. Iran, which has been unable to oust Saddam militarily, is undeniably counting on Iraq's economic problems to effect his removal.

While the Iranian economy has suffered badly as a result of the war, the accumulated consequences have not been as drastic for Iran as they have been for Iraq, mainly because of the Iranian regime's ability to expand its petroleum production by the fall of 1982 to its prewar level of 2.5–3 million barrels per day.[41] In the intervening two years, Iranian production had been 1–1.5 million barrels per day, and this had been a hardship for the country. It was precisely when Iran had managed to drive the Iraqi forces out of the country that it was able to expand its production and regain its position of prominence in OPEC, first forcing Saudi Arabia to reduce its output in order to protect the OPEC price structure and then, when these cutbacks were not enough, forcing OPEC in March 1983 to reduce its prices from $34 to $29 per barrel.[42] Iran itself was not really affected by this reduction, since it was already selling its oil at discount rates of between $24 and $29 per barrel.

Despite the increase in oil exports, the Iranian economy has failed to rebound to its prerevolutionary buoyancy, mainly because of war-related expenses. The economy was in an unhealthy condition at the beginning of the war. Iran's assets in the United States were frozen as a result of the hostage crisis, and it was being forced to pay higher prices for agricultural imports no longer available from the United States. The European and American economic boycott of Iran produced shortages of all types of goods. Furthermore, many middle-class members of the managerial sector had fled Iran because of the regime's puritanical policies, such as the banning of music and entertainment programs on television and radio and the requirement of the *hejab* (Islamic dress) for women. Added to the shortages of goods and managers was the shortage of refined fuel because of the Iraqi bombardment of the world's largest refinery in Abadan during the first days of the war. Consequently, Iran's gross domestic product for the year ending March 1981 decreased by 16.57 percent, according to the Iranian central bank, with annual unemployment of 12.7 percent.[43] While industrial production was reduced and unemployment was high, the government was faced with the task of caring for hundreds of thousands of refugees who had fled the Khuzestan war zone and descended on urban areas such as Shiraz, Isfahan, Tehran, and Qom. Furthermore, the exodus of peasants from rural to urban areas had continued after the fall of the shah; Tehran's population especially increased dramatically.[44]

The result of all this has been inflation. According to central bank data, consumer prices rose 23.55 percent in the year ending March 1981 (Bani-Sadr had estimated it to be 27 percent) and 25 percent in the year ending March 1982 (as much as 50 percent, according to the Economists' Society of Iran). From May 1982 through May 1983, prices rose another 20 percent according to the bank.[45] On the basis of these reports, considered very conservative by most observers, there has been about a 70 percent increase in consumer prices during the three years of the war.

Reports coming out of Tehran during the summer of 1983 indicate that prices for most goods have soared in the last six months, partly as a result of the liberalization program instituted by Khomeini last December, which removed prosecution for profiteering from the revolutionary courts and placed it with the Justice Ministry's public courts. For example, when rice was removed from the list of rationed items in early July, prices promptly doubled to 700 rials ($6.50 by the official exchange rate) a kilo, forcing many Iranians to switch to bread and causing long lines at bakeries.[46] The Syndicate of Islamic Bazaar Merchants has denied charges that its members are destroying the nation through profiteering and has countered by accusing the government, which it contends controls 90 percent of the nation's imports, of having caused the present inflation in Iran. They argue, for example, that while steel and butter prices went down on the world market in 1982-83, prices for these government-controlled items increased in Iran.[47] There has been some talk of returning the prosecution of profiteers to the much more stringent revolutionary courts. Whether or not that occurs, inflation will continue to be the curse of the Iranian economy as long as the war continues.

Conclusion

Iraq's initiation of hostilities was predicated on the assumption that dissatisfied elements within Iran would quickly depose the regime and reach an understanding with Iraq. That assumption having been proven wrong, Iraq sought the termination of hostilities. While the more liberal members of the Iranian regime, such as Bani-Sadr and former premier

Bazargan, wanted a termination of hostilities in order to achieve the goals of the revolution in Iran, the more ardent IRP members, such as Beheshti, Raja'i, and 'Ali Khamena'i (Khomeini's representative on the Council of Guardians and the present president of Iran), have vowed not to terminate the hostilities until an Islamic republic has displaced Saddam Hosain in Iraq. As early as January 1981, a close aide of Khomeini declared: "The Imam sees the war on the basis of a fixed strategy. This is continuing efforts to revive the great state of Islam, and the emergence of Islam as a third force to confront the East and the West."[48]

The fall of Bani-Sadr signaled the end of any possibility of a negotiated settlement with Iraq. Iran's ability to push back the Iraqis from its soil and continue the war has allowed Khomeini to consolidate the revolution at home; however, he has so far failed to export his Islamic Revolution to other states in the Middle East.[49] Iran is, of course, now hoping that the economic difficulties facing the present Ba'th leadership in Baghdad will foster enough domestic discontent to accomplish a change in regime. Saddam, however, has shrewdly eliminated all possible rivals within the Revolutionary Command Council that rules the country. A coup d'etat against him by the army also seems unlikely, since the senior officers are almost all Sunnis and are closely watched by the internal security apparatus.[50]

What seems more likely is that the present standoff will continue for some time. Iran, now economically ascendant, can afford to continue the hostilities against Iraq. The Tehran regime has suffered too much in lost life and property in the past three years suddenly to come to the negotiating table. It would be difficult to justify such a move to the Iranian public, since all the major Iranian officials have pledged not to do so.[51] Furthermore, the continuation of hostilities keeps alive Tehran's hope that Saddam will fall and an Islamic republic will rise in Iraq.

Saddam Hosain, realizing that the Tehran regime is intent on pursuing the war and cognizant of his country's increasing economic difficulties, has vowed to disrupt Iran's oil exports by bombing the Kharg Island loading terminals. Now that he is in possession of the Super Etendard aircraft equipped with Exocet missiles, his threats have become more credible. As of now (early November 1983) no damage has been done to the Kharg facilities, but Iraq has sunk a number of Iranian ships in the Gulf and supposedly mined the entrance to Bandar Khomeini Harbor. While these latter actions will be costly for Iran, they will not greatly hamper its ability to pursue its war effort as long as the Kharg Island facilities are not seriously damaged.

Alternatively, Saddam is seeking to increase Iraq's oil exports. While efforts to reopen the pipeline through Syria have proved futile, he has initiated the construction of additional pumping stations that will increase Iraqi oil exports piped through Turkey from 650,000 to 950,000 barrels a day.[52] Iraq has also signed a contract with a German firm to transport 140,000 barrels of oil daily over land to port facilities on the Red Sea in Saudi Arabia. Additionally, Saudi Arabia has given Iraq the right to use one of its underutilized pipelines. Saddam has announced that it will take between six months and a year to build a connecting pipeline from the Iraqi oil fields to the Saudi pipeline. Iraq is expected to export 1.1 million barrels of oil a day through this pipeline. Once these additional facilities are completed, Iraq's oil exports will be about 2,200,000 barrels a day, or over three times what it is now exporting. With this increased oil output, Iraq will once again have the financial resources to continue the hostilities. Unless either Iran or Iraq is able to cut off the other's oil exports, the war will continue to rob them of their soldiers, civilians, and resources.

Notes

1. For a detailed if somewhat biased (toward Iraq's position) discussion of Iran-Iraq relations, see Tareq Y. Ismael, *Iraq and Iran: Roots of Conflict* (Syracuse: Syracuse University Press, 1982), pp. 1–40.

2. "Algiers Declaration of March 6th, 1975: Joint Communiqué between Iran and Iraq," Ismael, *Iraq and Iran*, pp. 60–62.

3. "Interview between Shebli al-Aisani and Fred Halliday in April 1979 in Baghdad," *Merip Reports*, no. 97 (June 1981), p. 19.

4. Joe Stork, "Iraq and the War in the Gulf," *Merip Reports*, no. 97 (June 1981), p. 12.

5. Michael Hudson, *Arab Politics: The Search for Legitimacy* (New Haven: Yale University Press, 1977), pp. 2, 7.

6. Hanna Batatu, "Iraq's Underground Shi'i Movement." *Merip Reports*, no. 102 (June 1982), pp. 3–9. Saddam's concern over Khomeini's propaganda was understandable, given the almost total exclusion of the Shi'is from the upper ranks of the Iraqi Ba'th party. "Up to November 1963 it [the Ba'th party] had, to a large extent, the characteristic of a genuine partnership between the Sunni and Shi'i 'pan-Arab' youth. By 1968, however, the role of the Sunnis had risen sharply, while that of the Shi'is had decisively declined. Out of the total of fifty-three members of the top command that led the party from November 1963 to 1970, 84.9 percent were Sunni Arabs, 5.7 percent Shi'i Arabs, and 7.5 percent Kurds, whereas for the period 1952–November 1963, the comparable figures were 38.5; 53.8; and 7.7 percent. A similar process appears to have taken place in the intermediate and lower layers of the 'active membership.' This means, of course, that the party has become homogeneous, but at the same time less representative" (Hanna Batatu, *The Old Social Classes and the Revolutionary Movements of Iraq* [Princeton: Princeton University Press, 1978], p. 1078).

7. Claudia Wright, "Implications of the Iran-Iraq War," *Foreign Affairs*, Winter 1980–81, p. 278.

8. Ibid., pp. 280–81.

9. On Iraq's interpretation of the events leading to the war see Nicola Firzli, ed., *The Iraq-Iran Conflict* (Paris: Editions du Monde Arabe, 1981). See also *The Iraq-Iranian Conflict: Documentary Dossier* (Baghdad: Ministry of Foreign Affairs Publications, 1981), pp. 1–223.

10. Wright, "Implications of the Iran-Iraq War," p. 286. See also Stephen R. Grummon, *The Iran-Iraq War: Islam Embattled* (New York: Praeger, 1982), p. 14.

11. Grummon, *The Iran-Iraq War: Islam Embattled*, pp. 24–25. See also David Hirst, "Can Iran Avoid Defeating Itself?" *Manchester Guardian Weekly*, February 15, 1981.

12. Iran, however, was able to buy the spare parts it needed on the world market. Israel became the main source of parts for its American-made Phantoms. Syria, Libya, and North Korea have been its other main arms suppliers ("Syria Said Halting Arms Flights to Iran," *Iran Times*, October 1, 1982, p. 16; "Israel Says the United States Knew of Sales to Iran," *Iran Times*, October 29, 1982).

13. Eric Rouleau, "The War and the State," *Merip Reports*, no. 98 (July-August 1981), pp. 5–6; "Why War with Iraq Is Stiffening Iran's Morale," *World Business*, February 23, 1981. One of the main problems facing the Iranian armed forces initially was the rivalry and competition between the army and the Revolutionary Guards (Pasdaran). The IRP, doubtful of the army's (especially the officer corps') devotion to the revolution, insisted on the presence of Pasdaran in the various army units. The officers resented having to share authority with the Pasdaran, whom they viewed as inexperienced and foolhardy fanatics. They accused them of forcing the fighting units to take unnecessary chances, thus causing high casualties. The Pasdaran, in turn, viewed the army as not sufficiently aggressive. The animosity between the army and the Pasdaran eventually subsided, especially after the Iranians had expelled the Iraqis from Iran during the summer of 1982. The Pasdaran's role in human-wave attacks on the Iraqis had been instrumental in the Iranian victories. These attacks failed to give them victories, however, once they were on Iraqi soil, and this had a sobering influence on the Pasdaran, who have come to respect the advice of seasoned army officers. The Pasdaran now number a hundred fifty to two hundred thousand and boast their own mechanized units (Youssef Ibrahim, "Piety and Power: Iran's Clerics Tighten Grip by Instituting Islam in Every Detail of Life," *Wall Street Journal*, December 1, 1982, p. 1). The regular army is estimated to have two hundred thousand men.

14. Eric Rouleau, "The War and the State," pp. 3–4.

15. Sepehr Zabih, *Iran since the Revolution* (Baltimore: Johns Hopkins University Press, 1982), p. 53.

16. Ibid., chaps. 5 and 7.

17. Ibid., chap. 6.

18. "Bani Sadr Is Given Asylum in France," *New York Times*, July 29, 1981, pp. A1 and A3. See also Nikki R. Keddie, *Roots of Revolution* (New Haven: Yale University Press, 1981), p. 271.

19. "33 High Iranian Officials Are in Bombing at Party Meeting; Chief Justice Is Among Victims," *New York Times*, June 29, 1981, pp. A1 and A7.

20. "It Helps If You Are Ready to Die," *Economist*, December 25, 1981, pp. 42–43; Robert C. Toth, "Iran May Be Re-Emerging as Gulf Power," *Los Angeles Times*, January 25, 1982.

21. "Iran Says It Has Recaptured Port and Taken 30,000 Prisoners," *New York Times*, May 25, 1982, p. 1.

22. "Iraq Leaving Iran to Win Over Arabs," *Iran Times*, June 25, 1982, p. 16.

23. Roger Matthews and Reginald Dale, "Iran Invades Iraq in Bid to Topple Hussein," *Financial Times*, July 15, 1982.

24. "Iraqis Claim to Have Repelled Iran Advance," *Times* (London), October 7, 1982, p. 6.

25. Charles J. Hanley, "Iran Opens Offensive in Central Battle Area," *Washington Post*, November 3, 1982, p. 5.

26. Drew Middleton, "Iranian Drive on the Iraqis Called Failure," *New York Times*, February 19, 1983.

27. "Iran Oil Field in Gulf Raided, Iraq Claims," *Los Angeles Times*, March 3, 1983.

28. "Latest Offensive Languishes," *Iran Times*, April 22, 1983, p. 16.

29. "Iran Reports Major Advance in New Drive against Iraqis," *New York Times*, July 25, 1983, p. 3.

30. Drew Middleton, "Gulf War Threats to Oil Signal a Shift," *New York Times*, November 3, 1983, p. 12. The fact that Saddam sent his presidential guard to the Panjvin front is an indication of the vulnerability of Iraqi forces in the area.

31. For a full discussion of this issue, see Bruce Maddy-Weitzman, "Islam and Arabism: The Iran-Iraq War," *Washington Quarterly*, Autumn 1982, pp. 181–88.

32. Tareq Y. Ismael, *The Arab Left* (Syracuse: Syracuse University Press, 1976), chap. 2.

33. Alan R. Taylor, *The Arab Balance of Power* (Syracuse: Syracuse University Press, 1982), chap. 6.

34. "Troops from Sudan to Aid Iraq in War," *Times* (London), October 4, 1982, p. 4.

35. Karen Elliot House, "Iraq's Leaders, Choosing Guns Over Butter, Put the Brakes on Nation's Economic Development," *Wall Street Journal*, March 15, 1983, p. 56.

36. Patrick Cockburn, "Iraq Seeks Bank Credit to Fund Project," *Financial Times*, March 18, 1983.

37. The $20 billion figure is quoted by the Iraqi foreign minister, Tareq Aziz. U.S. government and congressional sources, however, estimate the figure to be above $30 billion (Peter Maass, "Oil Facilities Could Be Targeted: French Jets Seen Giving Iraq New Capability against Iran," *Washington Post*, July 31, 1983.

38. "Money and Motive in Short Supply," *Economist*, February 5, 1983, p. 17. According to *Time* (June 23, 1983), the Iraqis had depleted their gold reserves

by midsummer 1983. The *Washington Post* (August 2, 1983) reported that the Iraqi government had initiated a campaign to induce citizens to contribute their jewelry to the state in order to help pay for the war. According to the report, two tons of gold had been collected.

39. John M. Goshko and Ward Sinclair, "U.S. Offering Iraq Credits on Food Commodity Sales," *Washington Post*, February 16, 1983, p. A14.

40. The Ba'th leaders have worked hard to gain the allegiance of the Iraqi masses. They have instituted a land redistribution program in the countryside unburdened by redemption payments to landlords, electrified forty-two hundred villages, introduced health insurance for the peasantry, pushed toward the mechanization of agriculture, and succeeded in reclaiming over 4 million dunoms of land. Additionally, "they created 'people's markets,' enabling the peasants to sell the products of their labor at market prices through appropriate governmental agencies—the Institutions for the Grain Trade and the Dates Trade—without the interposition of middlemen. Over and above this, they have maintained by state subsidy the price of the popular loaf of bread at 6 fils; lowered the prices of all agricultural machines significantly and of chemical fertilizers by 50 percent; reduced the fees for state technical and advisory services to farmers by 30 to 50 percent; raised the minimum daily wage for unskilled workers in the public sector and the departments of government from 450 to 550 fils in 1973, to 650 fils in 1974, 900 fils in 1976 and 1100 fils in 1977; and extended social security and disability benefits to all industrial, transport, and contractual laborers and laborers in commercial houses—and not simply to laborers in establishments employing ten or more persons, as under an older law" (Batatu, *The Old Social Classes*, pp. 1095–96).

41. John Yemma, "How Gulf War Is Bad and Good for Some in Oil World," *Christian Science Monitor*, February 7, 1983, p. 5. See also Central Intelligence Agency, *International Energy Statistical Review* (Washington: U.S. Government Publications, January 31, 1984), p. 1.

42. "Iran Won't Do What It's Done," *Iran Times*, March 18, 1983, p. 12.

43. "Mullah's Tussle with Ravaged Economy," *Toronto Star*, July 17, 1983.

44. Tehran's population according to the 1976 census was 4.5 million and now approximates 7 million. Much of this 55 percent increase has occurred since the revolution in 1979. See Farhad Kazemi, *Poverty and Revolution in Iran* (New York: New York University Press, 1980), pp. 12–17, and Liz Thurgood, "Food Shortages Bite on Iran's Home Front," *Guardian*, July 30, 1983.

45. Patrick Clawson, "Iran's Economy: Between Crisis and Collapse," *Merip Reports*, no. 98 (July-August 1981), p. 12. See also "Inflation Up," *Iran Times*, July 22, 1983, p. 13.

46. Thurgood, "Food Shortages."

47. "The Import and Distribution of 90% of Overpriced Items Are in the Hands of Government," *Iran Times*, August 4, 1983, p. 5.

48. "How Iran's Leaders View War with Iraq," *Christian Science Monitor*, January 14, 1981.

49. Khomeini has not only been unsuccessful in exporting his Islamic Revolution, but also failed to achieve the main goal of the revolution in Iran,

improvement in the living conditions of the masses. One of the main reasons for this is, of course, the expense of the war. For example, the March 1983–March 1984 war budget, as announced by Mohammad Taqi Banki, the director of the Planning and Budget Organization, is between 50 and 60 billion tomans ("Because of the War the Islamic Republic Cannot Eliminate the Problems of Shortages and Goods and Long Lines," *Iran Times*, September 30, 1983, p. 4).

A more important reason for the continuing poverty of the masses in Iran, however, is the present regime's commitment to private property, which the regime declares to be sacrosanct in Islam. The failure of the Islamic Revolution to implement large-scale land redistribution, nationalize foreign trade, and secure dignified labor legislation is an indication of its bias toward the propertied class, despite its constant exhortation on behalf of the disinherited. The Islamic Revolution is more a conservative reaction against modernity than a genuine revolution which seeks to address the social and economic plight of the masses ("Trade Nationalization Is Un-Islamic," *Iran Times*, December 17, 1982, p. 16; Ahmad Ashraf, "Bazaar and the Mosque in Iran's Revolution," *Merip Reports*, no. 113 (March-April 1983), pp. 15–18.

50. A coup might conceivably be initiated by one of three groups within the army. The first consists of some twenty-five top Sunni generals from the same village as Saddam, Takriti, who have reached their present positions of eminence through religious, local, and blood ties with him. Members of this rather cohesive group realize that they will either rule together or fall together and are therefore unlikely to attempt a coup. (For a detailed discussion of the Takriti connection of the second Ba'th regime, see Batatu, *The Old Social Classes*, chap. 58.) The second comprises some two hundred fifty Sunni generals directly below the Takriti clique. Since they are exclusively Sunni and are closely watched by the state intelligence apparatus under Saddam's brother Barzan, it is unlikely, though not impossible, that a coup would arise from this quarter. The third is the lower ranks of the army, which is 60–70 percent Shi'i. This group, however, lacks the organizational capacity to bring down Saddam. There is, of course, the possibility that Shi'i enlisted men might refuse to fight if the military situation deteriorates further, but in the past the morale of Iraqi soldiers has improved when they have been defending their homeland against the Iranians and they have performed with distinction.

51. The death of Khomeini would not change things dramatically, since his replacements would most likely feel bound, because of his stature, to follow his policies concerning the war for some time (at least a year).

52. "Iraq May Have Scheme to Up Its Oil Exports," *Iran Times*, October 21, 1983, p. 15.

FARHAD KAZEMI

Iran, Israel, and the Arab-Israeli Balance

Iran's relationship with Israel and the Arab countries has been interesting and complex. Ever since the creation of the state of Israel, the Iranian government has tried to maintain some kind of balance in its interactions with the Israeli and Arab adversaries. Depending on the government in power and the intricacies of regional and international politics, the balance has tilted to one side or the other. It has, however, always been an unsteady and precarious equilibrium subject to internal and external pressures. The purpose of this paper is to analyze Iran's complex relationshp with Israel in the context of the Arab-Israeli conflict and relevant domestic and international considerations.

An important factor in Iran's relationship with Israel is the status of Iranian Jews and the historical evolution of the Jewish community under various Iranian dynasties. Changes in the status of the Jews have been effectively analyzed by many scholars.[1] I shall first briefly summarize these findings and then analyze the post–World War II developments in some detail.

The earliest account of the Jews in Iran, as related by Laurence Loeb,[2] is a legend about the accidental arrival in Iran of Serah bat Asher, a granddaughter of Jacob. According to the age-old story, Serah bat Asher was tending sheep in the Judean hills when a lamb strayed into a nearby cave. She pursued it, and when, after an arduous chase, she emerged at the other end of the cave, she found herself near present-day Isfahan. Written biblical and other accounts of Jewish settlements in Iran have been reported in the pioneering works of Walter Fischel and other scholars. One of the best-known events is Cyrus the Great's freeing of the Jews from exile in Babylonia and his restoration of the Temple at Jerusalem in 538 B.C. Other recorded evidence points to Jewish settlements in different corners of Iran at about the same period. Overall, the Jews of pre-Islamic Iran were accepted and allowed to practice their religion. There were, of course, occasional troubled times, most notably reflected in the story of Esther and Haman. The Jews were also subject to the intermittent hostility of Zoroastrian priests, the severity of which depended to a large extent on the personality of the reigning Sasanian monarch and the relative power of the priestly caste.

The Islamic conquest of Iran in A.D. 642 was not necessarily viewed as a calamity by the Jews. They were granted the status of protected minority (*dhemmi*) and partook of the cultural expansion and development of early Islamic civilization. They were, however, subjected to heavy taxation and probably also some of the prejudice directed against other non-Muslim and non-Arab elements of the population. Jewish settlements were established throughout the country in both urban and rural areas,[3] and the Jews engaged in a variety of occupations in commerce and trade. Isfahan emerged as the primary center of Jewish learning, but Talmudic scholarship was also in evidence in other parts of Iran.[4] Messianic movements emerged sporadically in Isfahan and elsewhere.

The available information on Jewish life in Iran during the centuries immediately preceding the Mongol invasion is not extensive, but a Jewish presence persisted in many areas of Iran. There is evidence of extensive activities by adherents of the Karaite schism in the ninth and tenth centuries. The Mongol invasion of the thirteenth century resulted in the destruction of several major cities and the massacre of their populations. The Jews, along with other Iranians, suffered heavily at the hands of the invaders. A few prominent Jews, however, emerged as key officials of the administration in the ensuing period. Some of them even reached the rank of grand vizier of the Il-Khanids and provided protection and a brief respite for their Jewish brethren. With the downfall of these officials, Jewish life once again suffered.

The coming to power of the Safavid dynasty in 1501 created a new situation for Iranian Jewry. The Safavids made Shi'ism the state religion and showed overwhelming zeal in transforming Iran into a Shi'i land. A new and more acute intolerance was directed against non-Shi'is and expressed with some regularity in persecutions of the Jews. Codes of conduct and rules designed to restrict Jewish social and economic life were promulgated.[5] Pressures for conversion were particularly strong and resulted in a decrease of the Jewish population and severe intra-communal strife. Special identifying clothing, their "badge of shame," was required of the Jews, further segregating them from the dominant Shi'i community. The Law of Apostasy allowed a Jewish convert to Islam to "inherit all of the property of his relatives, even those of distant degree."[6]

The restrictive codes of the Safavids, among the most severe in the Muslim world, had detrimental consequences for Jewish economic, social, legal, and political rights. As Sorour Soroudi remarks, the main purpose of these regulations was "to degrade the Jew in the eyes of the Muslim."[7] The only respite for the Jews came after the downfall of the Safavids, under Nader Shah Afshar (1736–47) and Karim Khan Zand (1750–79). With the establishment of the Qajar dynasty in late eighteenth century, however, many of the Safavids' restrictive codes, mass conversion pressures, and other forms of persecution were revived. The relative ascendancy of the Shi'i clerics in the Qajar era contributed to this rise in anti-Jewish sentiment. The Jews of Mashhad and Tabriz in particular suffered enormously during this period.[8] The general worsening of the situation was probably a factor in the conversion of many Jews to the new Babi-Baha'i religious movement.[9]

The Qajar period also heralded a few important positive developments for the Iranian Jews. First, communications and contacts with world Jewry were reestablished. Second, secular education was made available through the creation of the first *Alliance* school in 1898.[10] Finally, the adoption of a constitution based on popular representation in 1906 officially and formally recognized the Iranian Jews as a religious minority. The Jews were allowed to elect a representative to the Iranian parliament. Although these changes were slow in coming, they affected the community in a beneficial way.

The next notable event for Iranian Jewry was the coming to power of Reza Shah and the establishment of the Pahlavi dynasty in 1925. Reza Shah's programs of modernization and secular nationalism as well as the tight rein he imposed on clerical influence helped the Jewish community immensely. He abrogated the Law of Apostasy and abolished the *jezya* (poll tax).[11] Jews entered a variety of occupations, including government service. The only discontinuity in this period was Reza Shah's sympathy for the Axis powers, which eventually resulted in his forced abdication in favor of his son in 1941.

The succession of Mohammad Reza Pahlavi to the Peacock Throne greatly improved the status of the Jews in Iran. Despite sporadic anti-Jewish incidents and the anti-Baha'i campaign of 1955, his reign can probably be considered a "Golden Age" for minorities in modern Iran. The Jews prospered economically, socially, and culturally, especially in the last two decades of the shah's rule. A new and vigorous Jewish bourgeoisie emerged in the capital city, which in turn attracted Jewish migrants from provincial towns and rural areas. By the early 1970s, Tehran was the center of Jewish economic and social activities. Iran's Jewish population surpassed eighty thousand, with perhaps over half residing in Tehran.

During this period the Iranian Jews also benefited from the generally friendly and multifaceted relationship of Iran with Israel. This relationship went through different phases in the course of the shah's regime but on the whole permitted official governmental interactions and cordial, if discreet, diplomatic intercourse.

As a member of the United Nations Special Committee on Palestine, Iran was involved in issues concerning the creation of the state of Israel as early as 1947. The committee unanimously recommended the termination of the British mandate in Palestine. Its members were, however, divided on the question of Palestine's future. The majority recommended its partition into separate Jewish and Arab states. The minority, composed of Iran, India, and Yugoslavia, favored a federal state. Iran's vote on the partition resolution in the General Assembly was also negative. Similarly, Iran voted against Israel's admission to the United Nations on May 11, 1949.

Iran's actions were based on regional political considerations and sensitivity to the general sentiments of the Arab countries. They were also due in part to domestic politics and the influence of the Shi'i clerics, especially Ayatollah Abu'l-Qasem Kashani. Kashani and his followers from the fanatical Feda'iyyin-e Islam organized a major demonstration against Jews and Zionists involving several thousand participants in Tehran in May 1948. A proclamation condemning the Zionists in Palestine was issued, and volunteers were urged to sign up for duty on behalf of the Muslim Palestinian brothers. About five thousand men volunteered but were refused permission by the government to proceed to Palestine.[12]

In spite of this agitation at home, the Iranian government moved slowly to accommodate the new political reality in the Middle East. In March 1950, the government of Prime Minister Mohammad Sa'ed granted de facto recognition to Israel. This decision was reached by a unanimous vote of the cabinet without much fanfare. The first major public notice of the recognition decision was aired in two separate meetings of the Iranian Senate in late May and reported in the local press. A "special representative" was dispatched to Tel Aviv, and discussion of trade agreements was initiated by an Israeli delegation in Tehran.[13]

Israel's hope for de jure recognition did not materialize. The Anglo-Iranian oil dispute and nationalization of Iranian oil in 1951 created intense domestic turmoil. The grand coalition supporting oil nationalization included a significant clerical representation led by Kashani. The Iranian envoy in Tel Aviv was recalled, and no serious attempt at improving relations was made, although some trade negotiations continued during Prime Minister Mohammad Mosaddeq's era.[14]

The coup of August 1953 that restored the shah to the throne resulted in the gradual reestablishment of suspended ties with Israel. The extent and intensity of these ties increased to the point that the shah once described them as "like the true love that exists between two people outside of wedlock."[15] He publicly affirmed the recognition of Israel and the relationship between the two countries in a news conference in July 1960. The immediate repercussions of the announcement in the Arab world took the Iranians by surprise. President Nasser of Egypt denounced the Iranian ties and charged that "the Shah had shown a 'hostile attitude' toward Egypt, the United Arab Republic, the Arab Nations, and Arab nationalism since 1953."[16] The Jordanian premier expressed his government's regret over this matter. Similar comments were made by the Iraqis and an Arab League spokesman.[17] Nasser ordered the closure of the Egyptian embassy in Tehran. This was followed by a statement by the Arab League that the economic boycott of Israel might be extended to Iran. In a show of anger, the shah severed diplomatic relations with Egypt and recalled the Iranian ambassador from Cairo. The crisis reached its peak when the foreign minister of Iran described Nasser in a news conference as "this light-headed pharaoh who is ruling by bloodshed."[18] In the same gathering, the foreign minister reiterated that this was simply a de facto recognition that had remained unchanged for the past ten years.

The Arab reaction notwithstanding, Iranian-Israeli ties were solidified in the 1960s. These included a wide variety of political, economic, military, and strategic relationships. The unobtrusive Israeli "embassy" in Tehran was the focal point of most of the political contacts. The unmarked compound and the low profile of the Israeli diplomatic personnel kept their presence out of the public eye. Israeli delegates, however, regularly attended various international conferences held in Tehran and participated in athletic events, including the much publicized 1974 Asian Games. Furthermore, the airline El Al operated openly through the main concourse of Tehran's Mehrabad International Airport. As Marvin Weinbaum indicates, Iran's hospitality provided "Israel with backdoor respectability and legitimacy in the international community."[19]

Political contacts occasionally included visits by top Israeli government officials to the shah or other high-level Iranian politicians. Some of these visits are vividly described by Uri Loubrani, a former Israeli "ambassador" in Tehran, in several articles in the newspaper *Davar*, published after the downfall of the shah. Loubrani points out that "many Israeli leaders, in fact all the top political echelons since the establishment of the State, visited Tehran at one time or another. Among them were Ben Gurion, Golda Meir, Eban, Rabin, and Allon and—after the government changeover—Begin and Dayan too."[20] Dayan had made at least one other previous visit to Tehran, this one well-publicized, as the guest of the Iranian minister of agriculture, Hasan Arsanjani, in 1962.[21] Normally, however, these sojourns were quiet and secret affairs. In Loubrani's words:

The Iranians agreed to these meetings only on condition that it was promised in advance, that they would not be publicized. For their part, the hosts took care of the physical safety of the guest from Israel, for it was clear that if an Israeli personality were injured, an international scandal would ensue and all efforts to preserve the secrecy of the visits would be foiled. From the Israeli point of view, there was no need to keep these visits secret. We were careful about this only because we knew that if one visit became public knowledge, the Iranians would be hesitant about allowing another. Arrangements were, therefore, made in Israel so that the absence of the Israeli leader would not be noticed and invite guesses. This was the reason why the visits usually took place on the Sabbath or festivals.[22]

The economic connections were also extensive, ranging from oil transactions to agricultural assistance and consumer goods sales. Israelis provided the National Iranian Oil Company with technical assistance when production of Iranian oil was resumed in 1954 and sold to Israel, especially after the 1956 Suez campaign. The opening of the Strait of Tiran allowed routine delivery of Iranian oil through Elat. Israel's dependence on Iranian oil increased up until the 1967 capture of Egypt's Abu Rodais fields. Even after that date, Iranian oil continued to reach the Israeli market, though on a lesser scale. Furthermore, Iranians used the Elat-Ashdod pipeline to transport oil to European destinations.[23]

Israeli agricultural expertise provided another avenue for cooperation with Iran. Assistance in agricultural development, rural cooperative organization, and water resource administration was advanced by the Israelis through a number of agreements and contracts. The Qazvin area outside of Tehran became a focal point of much of the agricultural development activity. Israeli experts were contracted to rehabilitate the Qazvin villages after a powerful earthquake had devastated a large area in 1962.[24] Other contracts involving roads and buildings were also granted to Israeli corporations. Israeli consumer goods in modest amounts began to reach Iranian domestic markets in the 1970s.

Iranian-Israeli military and intelligence cooperation has received a fair amount of attention in media and other accounts. The full extent of these ties is not completely known. The available evidence points to Israeli technical assistance in the development of Iran's State Security and Intelligence Organization (SAVAK) in the late 1950s. Other forms of cooperation in military and security matters also existed. Exchange of intelligence items and joint operations among the Iraqi Kurds were apparently undertaken. Exchange of visits by military personnel and Israeli provision of advanced technical and electronic equipment were not uncommon. Some of these events were described by the shah's last air force chief, General Amir Hosain Rabi'i, as part of his defense before the Islamic Revolutionary Court. Asking for the court's mercy and clemency, Rabi'i gave the following account shortly before his execution:

> On the matter of visits to Israel, about 70 to 80 percent of military officers with the rank of major or higher made trips to Israel. Of the chiefs of staff, Azhari, Ovaisi . . . and air force chiefs frequently visited Israel. If they deny having gone to Israel, they are lying. I have been to Israel twice, once as a major and the second time as the chief of the air force. . . . The first trip was 15 years ago . . . where they showed us the Golan Heights and military bases. . . . In any event, visits to Israel were ordinary affairs. Every five to six months a group of officers were dispatched. . . . After receiving clearance from the J-2 branch, Israeli military personnel could also visit us. . . . The Israelis often tried to sell us electronic equipment and anti-radar devices. . . . Their chief of staff and the head of the air force would come and go. Most of their contracts were with our military and electronics division. . . . For repairs of airplanes and spare parts, they regularly contacted the Israelis.[25]

The bases of Israeli-Iranian cooperation in military and other matters during the shah's reign included the respective relationships of the two countries with the Arab governments, mutual intelligence and military benefits, Israeli military prowess and its demonstration against the Arabs, and the shah's perception of Iran's role and interest in the region. The relationship was cemented under the auspices and with the full knowledge of the United States government. The fact that both Iran and Israel relied heavily on the West, particularly the United States, facilitated cooperative ventures and made them reasonably predictable.

Aside from the perceived mutual benefits, another basis for the friendship and tacit alliance was, in Marvin Zonis's words, "rooted in their fundamentally marginal relationships to their neighbors."[26] The two countries shared marginal status and elements of insecurity and fear of Arab neighbors. As the perceptions of Arab threats mounted in the early 1960s, cooperation between Iran and Israel increased. A united Arab world led by a charismatic figure such as Nasser evoked pervasive fear in both the shah and the Israeli leaders. Paradoxically, the Israeli military success against the Arabs, particularly in the 1967 war, eroded and weakened some of the foundations of the perceived mutual interests.[27] Egypt was removed as a key threat to Iran. Moreover, the shah began to view Iran in the 1970s as a power to be reckoned with; he felt confident that he could handle Arab threats with relative ease.

Many of the ties between Iran and Israel remained in effect. Iran's official diplomatic positions, however, assumed a somewhat controlled and relatively pro-Arab posture. This revised diplomacy was often expressed in the context of the United Nations and in support of the positions of the more moderate Arab states. Aside from support for United Nations Resolution 242, diplomatic relations with Egypt were restored. Special friendly interactions with Jordan remained in force. Even the ubiquitous problems with Iraq were resolved as part of the Algiers Accord of 1975. In the 1973 war, medical aid was granted to Egypt and Syria, and Soviet planes were permitted to fly over Iranian air space.[28] Iran could also find other justifications for its revised posture vis-à-vis some Arab neighbors, among them extensive historical and cultural links with the Arabs, the common heritage of Islamic civilization, domestic religious and other opposition to strong ties with Israel, and the presence of a significant Arabic-speaking minority in Khuzestan and the Gulf area. Nevertheless, the Iranian vote in support of the Zionism/racism resolution in the General Assembly in 1975 may have taken the Israelis by surprise.

The onset of the Iranian revolution in the late 1970s resulted in a significant shift in Iran's relationship with Israel. One of the first concrete actions after the revolution's victory was the severing of relations with Israel in 1979. This was followed by Yaser Arafat's visit to Tehran as the first major foreign dignitary. Arafat was openly welcomed by Ayatollah Ruhollah Khomeini and was told by him that "Iran's revolution would be incomplete until the Palestinians won theirs."[29] Khomeini permitted the Palestine Liberation Organization to open a mission in Tehran in the former Israeli embassy. Additional missions were also installed in Ahvaz and Khorramshahr, both in oil-rich Khuzestan. Finally, Hani al-Hasan, a member of the more conservative Islamic wing of Fatah, was selected as the PLO representative in Iran.[30]

The pro-Arab and anti-Israeli shift in the revolutionary government was clear-cut. Israel was identified as evil and corrupt and a by-product of American imperialism. Khomeini officials lost no time in denouncing the Israelis and forecasting the future Islamic victory in Jerusalem over the "forces of evil." Clearly, the Iranian Jewish community was perturbed by these developments. The execution of the well-known Jewish businessman Habib Elqanian as a Zionist spy and for sowing "corruption on earth" greatly increased the fears of Iranian Jewry. Any form of contact with Israel could now be viewed ex post facto as a criminal act.[31] These fears were magnified whenever top Shi'i clerics failed to make a distinction between Judaism and Zionism. Some of the pronouncements also had anti-Semitic overtones. Khomeini's *Islamic Government*, for example, on several occasions refers to the Jews in ways that can be readily construed as anti-Semitic. He calls for the reinstitution of the jezya on non-Muslims and declares that if Muslims had obeyed divine ordinances "a handful of Jews would not have dared to occupy our land."[32] Describing the duties of the clerics, he lashes out at many groups, particularly the Jews:

> you have noticed in the traditions that the Messenger's successors, the Islamic jurists, are instructed to "teach the people"—that is, to teach the people their religion. This is especially significant under the current situation where the imperialistic politics and oppressive and traitorous rulers—the Jews, Christians, and materialists—attempt to distort the truths of Islam and lead the Muslims astray. Under these circumstances, our obligation for propagation and instruction is greater than ever. We see today that the Jews, may the curse of God be upon them, have violated the Quran and have altered its text published in the occupied territories. We are obligated to prevent their traitorous alterations. We must protect and make the people aware so that it becomes apparent that the Jews and their foreign supporters are against the foundations of Islam and want to establish a Jewish government in the world. Since they are a sly and energetic group, I fear (God forbid) that they may succeed. The weakness shown by us may permit a Jewish ruler to govern over us. May God never bring about such a day.[33]

To assuage some of the Jews' fears, certain overtures were made to them. A meeting was arranged in April 1979 between Khomeini and a delegation of Iranian Jews.[34] According to reports, Khomeini assured the group that they were part of the Iranian nation and would be treated with fairness if they did not associate with Zionists and oppressors of Islam. Furthermore, the new constitution of the Islamic Republic allowed for representation of the Jews in Parliament as an officially recognized religious minority.

These assurances were soon countered by the presentation to Parliament in 1981 of an Islamic code of retribution (*Layeha-ye Qesas*). This "Bill of Vengeance" views crime as a violation of the private rights of the victim or his heirs. It institutes specific procedures and regulations for receiving individual satisfaction for criminal acts. Relying heavily on witnesses and testimony, the plaintiff may receive monetary compensation (blood money) or, depending on the nature of the crime committed, exact execution. The law's Islamic thrust tends to discriminate against religious minorities. This is sometimes evident in the weight given to the testimony of non-Muslims in cases of crime or by omission of non-Muslims from many of the specific articles. Article 23 is particularly troublesome in that it withholds the right of "vengeance" from victims who have profaned the Prophet, his daughter Fatema, or the twelve Shi'i Imams. These restrictions can easily be abused by perpetrators of crimes against non-Muslims.

Members of the Iranian Jewish community and many others objected to aspects of this bill.[35] The protests were of no avail, and the essential features of the "Bill of Vengeance," with some modifications and time restrictions, received parliamentary approval in 1982. The potential impact of this law is vast; it fundamentally alters many of the basic precepts and norms of Iranian society. The effect on non-Islamic communities is even greater. It restricts some of their rights and makes due process and attainment of justice more difficult for them. It is, therefore, not surprising that the number of Jewish emigrants has increased since the inception of the Islamic Republic. The Jews have left primarily for Israel and the United States, although important pockets are also found in Western Europe.[36] The number of Jews still living in Iran has dwindled to approximately forty thousand, about half the prerevolution number.

On the official governmental level, Israel is regularly and vociferously attacked. The leaders of Israel are identified as tools of imperialism who do the bidding of the Great Satan, the United States. However, there is some inconclusive evidence that since the outbreak of the Iran-Iraq War, Iranians have purchased limited amounts of military spare parts indirectly from Israel. These relationships have been alluded to by Ariel Sharon and others in various media accounts. President Carter's national-security advisor Zbigniew Brzezinski notes this development in his recently published memoirs. In a section discussing the hostage crisis and the impact of the Iran-Iraq War on the eventual release of the American hostages, Brzezinski discusses the arms sale to Iran:

> It was at this juncture that we learned, much to our dismay, that the Israelis had been secretly supplying American spare parts to the Iranians, without much concern for the negative impact this was having on our leverage with the Iranians on the hostage issue. Muskie and I discussed this at some length and decided that the Secretary would make a strong demarche to the Israelis, since this was obviously undercutting our sensitive efforts. He did so, and, as far as I know, at least for a while the Israelis held back.[37]

The full extent of these sales and other forms of contact between Iran and Israel is not known. These contacts probably emerged at about the same time as the Iran-Iraq War, which increased Iran's need for arms and other matériel. The war affected Iran's regional position and brought home to the leaders of the revolution the necessity of an effective and well-organized armed force. It resulted in a resurgence of Iranian nationalism and stressed the urgency of defending the homeland against outsiders. It may have also rekindled negative attitudes toward Arabs among certain segments of the Iranian population. The fact that the

Gulf regimes provided Iraq with generous financial support was resented. About the same time, ties with the Palestinians began to weaken somewhat. Israel emerged, at least for the time being, as a beneficiary of Iran's new problems with the Arab countries. The war allowed for a limited pragmatic and indirect military relationship between Iran and Israel.

The foregoing account illustrates the complexity of Iran's relationships with its Jewish population, Israel, and the Arabs. The establishment of the Islamic Republic has created a new and more difficult milieu for Iranian Jewry. Certain social and legal rights of non-Muslims have been restricted in the regime's all-out drive toward Islamization of the social order. Moreover, any form of contact with coreligionists in Israel is by definition suspect and potentially damaging. What the future will bring for the indigenous Jewish population remains to be seen. At least at this juncture, the prospects are not bright. It is likely, however, that the ancient Jewish community of Iran will survive and find a way to cope with the social and legal limitations that are gradually being imposed on non-Muslims.

On the governmental level, possibilities for the reestablishment of Iran-Israel relationships similar to those of the shah's time are practically nonexistent. This does not mean that Iran will find its relationship with the Arab regimes satisfactory or mutually beneficial. Tensions between Iran and the Arab governments are likely to remain, in different forms and degrees, even after the termination of the Iran-Iraq War. In many ways, Iran's relationships with Israel and the Arabs resemble the swing of a pendulum. There is a basic steady middle course that is normally in some kind of balance but subject to pressures from the domestic and regional environment. The pendulum has swung to one side or the other depending on the particular Iranian regime's definition of its interest. If history teaches us any lesson, it is that, in the long run, Iran is unlikely to remain permanently at either extreme.

Notes

1. Walter Fischel, "The Jews of Persia: 1795–1940," *Jewish Social Studies* 12 (1950):119–60; idem, "Israel in Iran," in *The Jews: Their History, Culture, and Religion*, 3d ed., ed. Louis Finkelstein, 3 vols. (New York: Harper and Row, 1960), 2:1149–90; Sorour Soroudi, "Jews in Islamic Iran," *Jerusalem Quarterly* 21 (Fall 1981):99–114; Habib Levi, *Tarikh-e Yahud-e Iran*, 3 vols. (Tehran: Brukhim, ca. 1962). See also Shlomo Deshen and Walter Zenner, eds., *Jewish Societies in the Middle East: Community, Culture, and Authority* (Washington, D.C.: University Press of America, 1982).

2. Laurence Loeb, *Outcaste: Jewish Life in Southern Iran* (New York: Gordon and Breach, 1977), p. 274. See also J. Neusner, "Jews in Iran," in *Cambridge History of Iran*, vol. 3, pt. 2, *Seleucid, Parthian, and Sasanian Periods*, ed. Ehsan Yarshater (Cambridge: Cambridge University Press, 1983), pp. 909–23; Shaul Shaked, ed., *Irano-Judaica: Studies relating to Jewish Contacts with Persian Culture throughout the Ages* (Leiden: Brill, 1982).

3. Loeb, *Outcaste*, p. 279.

4. Ibid., p. 280, citing Walter Fischel, "Isfahan: The Story of a Jewish Community in Persia," in *Joshua Starr Memorial Volume* (New York: Jewish Social Studies Publication, 1953), p. 116. On the contribution of Iranian Jews to Persian literature of both pre- and post-Islamic periods, see Jalal Matini, "Ahamiyyat-e Athar-e Adabi-ye Farsi-ye Yahudian," *Iran Nameh* 1 (1983):424–46.

5. Soroudi, "Jews in Islamic Iran," p. 103.

6. Loeb, *Outcaste*, pp. 286, 292; Soroudi, "Jews in Islamic Iran," pp. 104–6; Fischel, "Israel in Iran," pp. 1167–71.

7. Soroudi, "Jews in Islamic Iran," p. 104.

8. Ibid., p. 106; Marvin Weinbaum, "Iran and Israel: The Discreet Entente," *Orbis* 18 (1975):1071.

9. See Walter Fischel, "The Bahai Movement and Persian Jewry," *Jewish Review*, March 1934, pp. 47–55; Hayyim Cohen, *The Jews of the Middle East: 1860–1972* (New York: Wiley, 1973), pp. 162–63.

10. Cohen, *Jews of the Middle East*, pp. 53–54, 141–46; S. Landshut, *Jewish Communities in the Muslim Countries of the Middle East* (Westport, Conn.: Hyperion Press, 1950), p. 65.

11. Loeb, *Outcaste*, p. 289; Soroudi, "Jews in Islamic Iran," p. 107.

12. Farhad Kazemi, "The Fada'iyan-i Islam: Fanaticism, Politics, and Terror," in *From Nationalism to Revolutionary Islam: Essays on Social Movements in the Contemporary Near and Middle East*, ed. Said Amir Arjomand (Albany: State University of New York Press, 1983), p. 162.

13. Weinbaum, "Iran and Israel," p. 1073.

14. Ibid., p. 1074, n. 10.

15. *Jerusalem Post*, December 31, 1961, quoted in Weinbaum, "Iran and Israel," p. 1070.

16. *New York Times*, July 27, 1960, p. 5.

17. *New York Times*, July 25, p. 2; July 27, p. 5; July 29, p. 1; August 1, p. 7; and August 30, p. 2, all 1960.

18. *New York Times*, July 28, 1960, p. 5.

19. Weinbaum, "Iran and Israel," p. 1077. Detailed analysis of Iran-Israel relations can be found in Samuel Segev, *The Iranian Triangle: The Secret Relations between Israel-Iran-U.S.A.* (Tel Aviv: Maariv, 1981). According to Segev (p. 94), El Al was permitted to operate in Iran in 1958 but only discreetly. After Nasser's death in 1970, El Al was allowed to function openly and advertise its flights. See also pp. 77–78, 80. I am indebted to David Menashri for sending me a copy of this book. I am also grateful to Shaul Bar for the time he took to read and translate the Hebrew text for me.

20. *Davar*, April 20, 1980, pp. 3–4.

21. Segev, *Iranian Triangle*, p. 108; Weinbaum, "Iran and Israel," p. 1076.

22. *Davar*, April 20, 1980, pp. 3–4. Segev points out that the Iranian foreign minister, 'Abbasqoli Khal'atbari, visited Israel in 1977 (*Iranian Triangle*, p. 153).

23. Discussion of the Iran-Israel oil link can be found in Robert Reppa, Sr., *Israel and Iran* (New York: Praeger, 1974), pp. 73–86; Segev, *Iranian Triangle*, p. 75; Weinbaum, "Iran and Israel," pp. 1078–80; Marvin Zonis, "Israel and Iran: From Intimacy to Alienation," *Moment* 4 (March 1979):13.

24. For details see Reppa, *Israel and Iran*, pp. 98–99.

25. Rabi'i's defense is (to my knowledge) part of the only published report of the proceedings of the Islamic Revolutionary Courts. Most of the minutes of the trial were published in Iranian newspapers. Three issues of *Ettela'at* give reasonable verbatim accounts of the trial: Farvardin 21, 22, and 23, 1358/1979. See also Segev, *Iranian Triangle*, pp. 72–74.

26. Zonis, "Israel and Iran," p. 12.

27. Ibid., p. 15.

28. Weinbaum, "Iran and Israel," p. 1081; Segev, *Iranian Triangle*, pp. 119, 176, 187.

29. John Cooley, "Iran, the Palestinians, and the Gulf," *Foreign Affairs*, summer 1979, p. 1017.

30. Ibid.

31. For a firsthand account of the Jewish community's distress at this time, see Barbara and Barry Rosen (with George Feifer), *The Destined Hour: The Hostage Crisis and One Family's Ordeal* (Garden City, N.Y.: Doubleday, 1982), pp. 78–80.

32. Ayatollah Ruhollah Khomeini, *Velayat-e Faqih: Hokumat-e Eslami* (Tehran, 1977), p. 38; also p. 6.

33. Ibid., p. 175.

34. During the first presidential elections held in the Islamic Republic, in January 1981, a radio reporter was dispatched to a Jewish activities center to interview the Jews and broadcast their views on the election. The reporter asked those present about the primary qualifications for the office of the president. Every respondent began with the statement that he must be a believing and true Muslim who respects, fulfills, and enforces Islamic injunctions.

35. A letter of protest was sent to members of Parliament by a group of Iranian Jewish intellectuals in April 1981.

36. Many of these recent Jewish immigrants to Israel are of modest socio-economic background and have practically no knowledge of Hebrew. For a variety of reasons, their adjustment to Israeli society has been difficult. There is, however, an organization of Iranian Jews in Israel. The organization was founded in 1979 and is led by the Iranian-born Likud member of the Knesset Moshe Katsav. The group arranges social and cultural activities and publishes *Payam*, a monthly Persian-language magazine that includes general articles on world events and Iranian Jewry, short stories, and other features. See, for example, *Payam* for August and November 1980.

37. Zbigniew Brzezinski, *Power and Principle: Memoirs of the National Security Adviser, 1977–1981* (New York: Farrar, Straus and Giroux, 1983), p. 504.

Iran and the
Strategic Rivalry in the Region

BARRY RUBIN

The State of U.S.-Iran Relations

In a television interview in January 1983, Iran's ambassador to the United Nations Sa'id Raja'i Khorasani stated, "The kind of relations we have with the United States are exactly what the people of Iran want. They are perfect. And they are altogether a lack of relations. In the future, I hope the situation will remain the same." The ambassador's remarks are typical of the views held by most Iranian leaders. They help to illustrate a relatively rare situation in international affairs, one in which the usual premises of diplomacy are turned upside down. One government wants no relations at all with another government, and time-honored routines such as the application of political or economic leverage, deterrence, and negotiation simply do not work. Any discussion of past or future interactions between the United States and the Islamic Republic of Iran must take this into account.

Raja'i Khorasani continued, "We believe that America is the center for world imperialism. Even though we have great respect for the American people, we however cannot respect the American government. We can under no circumstances trust them." After all, Ayatollah Ruhollah Khomeini himself said, "America is the enemy of God, the enemy of Islam, and the enemy of mankind."[1] Khomeini's dictum "The United States is the source of all our problems" characterizes many Iranian descriptions of historical and contemporary events. Marking the third anniversary of the taking of the U.S. hostages, Hojjat al-Eslam Asghar Musavi Kho'ini said, "It was under American orders that the Imam [Khomeini] was exiled, and it was American rifles that killed the students." Of the U.S. embassy, he added, "This building behind me was the center of the American spy network in the Middle East." Kho'ini concluded, "Now we have expelled these devils forever from our land."[2] The speaker of the Majlis, Hojjat al-Eslam 'Ali Akbar Hashemi Rafsanjani, claimed in December 1982, "Today we don't make any decisions, great or small, under the influence of foreign powers and a blasphemous country like the Soviet Union or an imperialist aggressive country like America."[3] About the same time, Oil Minister Gharazi told reporters that Iran would "never" knowingly sell oil to America, although U.S. oil companies are already buying oil and supplying technical assistance.

Iran's extreme bitterness toward the United States has both real and illusory causes. American support for the shah, particularly in the coup of 1953 and in training the SAVAK secret police, is a clear source of friction. Again, the United States encouraged the shah—although it scarcely ordered him as the Islamic revolutionaries would have it—to build up his armed forces and to buy large amounts of military equipment. The impact of Western, and particularly American, culture produced changes in Iran that are unpalatable from the Islamic viewpoint. U.S. companies on a number of occasions cheated the Iranian government. Other issues and activities could be cited.[4] On the other hand, the conspiracy theories of Iranian émigrés and leaders are grounded in illusion. If some U.S. policy makers have overestimated the role that Washington *could* play in affecting Iran's internal affairs, Iranians vastly overstate the role that Washington *did* play. The shah existed, wielded power in Tehran, and—no matter what one thinks of his policies—held his own nationalist vision. Subservience to the United States was certainly not his intention or his objective. He was to a considerable degree in control of his own destiny. His fall is attributable overwhelmingly to internal causes, neither brought about by nor easily preventable by U.S. action.

The Iranian perception of the United States as the "Great Satan," like most devil theories, rests on a grossly simplified stereotype, but this view is firmly held. Although it provides the Iranian leadership with a scapegoat, it is not consciously created or manipulated. Belief in virtually omnipotent foreign powers as the shapers of events has historically been an important manifestation of Iranian political culture. To argue that anti-Americanism will disappear because it is not functional in maximizing Iranian interests is to expect a degree of abstract rationality that does not often characterize the policies even of Western governments. The centrality of anti-Americanism in Iran today must be considered on its own "merits." The key question is whether Khomeini has fostered a permanent "cultural revolution" in Iranian attitudes, dismantling the traditional view that powerful foreign states must be appeased and rooting out the inferiority complex that has stirred Iranian resentment of foreigners. A Spanish journalist after a recent visit to Iran was quoted as saying of Iranians, "They are taught to hate Americans, taught that America is responsible for all their problems, and yet they're desperate for your approval." An Iranian disillusioned with the revolution told foreign reporters, "It will take time, and the new relationship will have to be less one-sided, but the animosity between our countries will not outlive Khomeini by much."[5]

While Khomeini's attitudinal revolution may not last forever, it can be expected to persist throughout the lifetime of the Islamic clerical regime. Only in 1982 did most Western observers come to accept the stability of the revolutionary regime and the viability—at least in the medium term—of its nonalignment policy. On the American side, the first assumption to be called into question was that of geopolitical determinism. Faced with a powerful Soviet Union along its northern border, ran this argument, Tehran would soon need to obtain U.S. support or run the risk of Soviet domination. Yet if Iranian nationalist Mohammad Mosaddeq in the early 1950s could develop a theory of superpower equilibrium consisting of good relations with both the Soviet Union and the United States, Khomeini could construct a notion of balanced hostility. Since the interest of each great power dictated preventing its rival from increasing its influence in Iran, Khomeini could abuse both and keep them at arm's length while still enjoying the benefits of nonalignment.

By 1982, when the Tehran regime had defeated the challenge of oppositionist guerrillas and begun to roll back the Iraqi forces, its ability to survive had become clear. With the destruction of the Tuda (Communist) party in 1983, its unwillingness to become too closely tied to the Soviet Union was also apparent. Finally, the failure of the Islamic Revolution to spread elsewhere had thrown into doubt the possibility that Iran would destabilize the Arab oil-producing states. U.S. policy makers began to realize that they would have to cope with a hostile Islamic regime for some time to come. At the same time, however, they now viewed this regime as having only limited capacity for disrupting the region. Only at this point did it become possible to construct a viable policy toward the problems raised by the Iranian revolution.[6]

These conclusions do not imply either an apologia for Iran's government—whose shortcomings, errors, and repressions have cost the Iranian people dearly—or any idea that the U.S. government is now supporting the Tehran government, overtly or covertly. The point here is simply that, despite the likely continued suspension of relations, the United States will have to deal with two issues raised by the changed situation in Iran and in the area. As so often happens in international relations, these two issues require somewhat contradictory responses. Briefly stated, the first is that the U.S. national interest requires the preservation of Iran's independence and sovereignty against any extension of Soviet control or influence. The second is that the U.S. interest requires the support of Gulf Arab allies against subversion, attack, or instability produced by Iranian attempts to extend their influence or their Islamic Revolution. It is easy to overstate the likelihood or danger of these threats, and overreaction is often counterproductive. Nevertheless, this is the framework within which American policy must operate.

To state the matter bluntly, the United States wants an Iran strong enough to resist Soviet overtures—and this is certainly the intention of the existing government in Tehran—but not so powerful as to threaten its Arab neighbors. The first of these aims is the more fundamental and requires not the maximization of U.S. influence (unlikely at present in any case) but the minimization of that of the Soviets. This holds true no matter how anti-American the Tehran government and how poor bilateral relations remain. Over time, a belief on the part of Iranians that the United States is indifferent to their fate could lead to a defeatist stance in relation to Moscow. Historically, Iranians (unlike the Afghans, who have fought rather than accommodated foreign powers) have tried to join the winning side. Whether Khomeini's emphasis on self-reliance has foreclosed for Iranian politicians the option of seeking secret U.S. or Soviet help in internal power struggles remains to be seen. Indeed, it may be in the U.S. interest to encourage Iranian nonalignment— certainly as preferable to Iranian-Soviet entente. The mass anti-Americanism so central to Iran's domestic political situation since the revolution precludes any easy reestablishment of ties as long as Khomeini lives and probably as long as his Islamic Republican Party (IRP) holds power. The Bazargan government's hesitant steps toward detente produced the radicals' takeover of the U.S. embassy in November 1979. The idea that economic difficulties or Soviet pressure will force Iran back into the Western camp is highly questionable.

The primary U.S. interest in Iran is the same as it has been since 1946—to support the country's independence, unity, and sovereignty so that it will continue to bar Soviet expansion. Direct or indirect extension of Soviet influence over Iran would threaten the vital Gulf region, with its massive petroleum reserves and key strategic crossroads. A secondary interest, before the current world oil glut made it less important, was the continued free flow of Iranian petroleum. Over the last three years the world has learned to get along with low Iranian production. The U.S. concern is not with Iran's oil but with the security of oil fields in Kuwait, Saudi Arabia, and elsewhere on the Gulf's southern shore.

If the revolution failed to change the historic U.S. interest in Iran, established at the cold war's dawn, it did reverse the new set of interests established in the early 1970s. At that time, the United States wanted a well-armed and active Iran as a bulwark against Soviet-supported radical forces in the region and as protector of the seemingly fragile Arab states across the Gulf. Now Iran has become a destabilizing force in its own right. Arab concern over Iran was heightened in 1981 by the discovery of Iran-trained revolutionaries, some of them Saudis, in Bahrain, seeking to overthrow Arab governments. Iran's relatively good battlefield performance against Baghdad and warnings to countries supporting Iraq are further worries. Thus, Iran has given the Arab countries an incentive to seek Western aid and regional self-defense cooperation.

Iran's threat has had a much more immediate effect on the Gulf states than has the seemingly more distant Soviet invasion of Afghanistan. The United States has no choice but to support a de facto alliance opposing any spread of Iranian influence or Islamic radicalism into the conservative Arab states. Knowledge of this fact inevitably builds continued anti-American sentiment in Iran. All of these factors pose tremendous difficulties for U.S. policy. America's desire that Iran be strong enough to oppose—even for its own Islamic radical reasons—expansion of Soviet power southward conflicts with its efforts to prevent the strengthening of Iran's regional position.[7]

Hostile relations between Washington and Tehran and the Iranian tendency to view both superpowers as evil but the United States as the greater evil mean at best noncooperation between the two—even if both are opposed to Soviet efforts—and at worst some parallel objectives between Tehran and Moscow. To understand this last danger better, one need merely consider Iran's similarity in world view—though opposite alignment—to the People's Republic of China. Beijing's equation of the Soviet Union and the United States has not prevented it from tilting toward the latter as the lesser evil.

The Iranian regime's political legitimacy has rested heavily on a single elderly man, but other leaders have worked hard to build a structure that will survive his passing.[8] While Khomeini's charisma provided its foundation, the IRP government has found ways to consolidate its position. Neighborhood committees, Islamic courts, the Revolutionary Guards, the SAVAMA intelligence corps, the "Party of God" street gangs, and other groups have supplied support and information for the regime from throughout the society. Anti-American and anti-Iraqi patriotism has provided an additional dimension of backing. The government's opponents are weak and divided.

Economically, while the shah's development programs came to a grinding halt, Iran has managed to limp along as an oil welfare state. As long as the country can produce over 2 million barrels of oil a day for export—even when it has to give sizable discounts to attract business—it can earn enough for necessary imports, including weapons. Petroleum income has also to some extent cushioned high rates of unemployment and inflation, although it has been unable to prevent rising dissatisfaction with living standards.[9]

By 1982-83, Iran held the upper hand in the Iran-Iraq War but was unable to achieve a decisive military victory. Iranian soil was cleared of Iraqi troops, but Khomeini still insisted on destroying the Baghdad regime. As the costly war dragged on, its political advantage for the Tehran government diminished. Still, the armed forces were kept busy with nonpolitical concerns, and battlefield victories were portrayed as proof of the revolution's efficacy.

The existing political forces are best divided into two categories: those inside and those outside the Islamic Republic framework. The key question in assigning a group to one or the other category is whether it would be likely to maintain, if it came to power, the broader structure of Islamic revolutionary ideology and policy and whether it shares to some degree in the legitimacy and distribution of power of the incumbent regime.[10] The three groups outside the framework are the émigrés, the left, and the ethnic minorities.

The émigrés are badly divided among themselves and have lost much of their base in Iran through flight, execution, purges, and the shift in the political spectrum. Their constant predictions of a quick triumph and the collapse of the Tehran government remain unfulfilled.

Much of the left is also in exile. There are three major leftist groups: the outlawed pro-Soviet Communists (Tuda), the Mojahedin-e Khalq, and the Feda'iyyin-e Khalq, the last of these split into at least two quarreling factions. The Tuda supported the government until it was crushed by massive arrests in the spring of 1983. The Mojahedin and a number of smaller groups conducted guerrilla warfare against the IRP from 1981 on and managed to assassinate many key figures in the government.[11] Yet the relative ease with which the IRP defeated the Mojahedin guerrillas and rounded up much of the Tuda's membership showed how limited a base the left possessed. Given the regime's monopolization of Islam and Khomeini's charisma, opponents are at a distinct disadvantage.

The ethnic minorities have had varied relations with the Islamic regime. The Arabs of the southwest failed to rally to the Iraqi invaders and seem unlikely to emerge as a political force; the Baluchis of the southeast and the nomadic tribes dislike, as always, central government rule but have caused relatively little trouble. The Turkish-speaking Azeris of the northwest rallied behind their respected religious leader, Ayatollah Kazem Shari'atmadari, but have at least for the present been broken by repression and by his house arrest in Qom. The Kurds, under the leadership of the Kurdish Democratic Party (KDP), which is allied with Kurdish Marxist groups, have waged an armed struggle tying down government troops and holding some "liberated" territory, but this resistance is divided and the government appears to hold the initiative. The KDP is now aligned with the Paris-based National Resistance Council (Bani-Sadr and the Mojahedin) but has made some overtures to the Soviets. Disillusionment with the United States for abandoning the Iraqi Kurds in 1975 after having supported them in a war against Baghdad makes the KDP wary of cooperation with Washington. Given the minorities' primary interest in their own regions, they will be only secondary factors in any Tehran power struggle. Ironically, the weakness of the central government has helped keep the provinces quiet, since the locals have been left alone to a far greater extent than in the shah era. The central government has, however, been fairly successful in imposing its will since the beginning of 1982. After the Iran-Iraq War, the IRP regime is likely to consolidate its hold on the provinces and impose a centralization of authority as the shah's father did in the 1920s. This could stir up regionalist feelings and offer opportunities for the Soviets or the United States to provide covert aid to the Kurds, the Azeris, the Baluchis, and the pastoral tribes, but this is not likely to have any major impact on Iranian life.[12]

The Islamic establishment includes the three IRP factions—the Maktabi, the Hojjatiyya, and the Mojahedin-e Islam—and the "traditionalist" clerics, the regular armed forces, and the Revolutionary Guards. These are likely to be the key groups in the struggle for power in Iran in the post-Khomeini period.

The Maktabi, whose members call themselves the "followers of the Imam's (i.e., Khomeini's) line," includes the current president and prime minister. It has been careful to support Khomeini's position in every detail, as well as land reform and other more radical social measures.

The more socially conservative and anticommunist Hojjatiyya has Mahdavi Kani, briefly prime minister, as its best-known figure. It seems to be the source of reports in the U.S. media of pro-Soviet sentiments among the Maktabi, something that says less about the Maktabi than about the possible willingness of the Hojjatiyya to seek Western support in the event of a showdown.[13]

The Mojahedin-e Islam is in many ways a grouping of independents. Many of them joined the antishah struggle relatively late. They are often a swing vote in the IRP, but the poor revolutionary credentials of many would probably bar them from power in their own right.

The membership and political positions of these factions often change, and it is hard to make definitive statements about them. While they cooperate closely at present, they might find it more difficult to stick together in a post-Khomeini situation. This is why the Maktabi has pressed for an early choice of Ayatollah Montazeri, who lacks Khomeini's stature and popularity, as successor to Khomeini's position. There are indications that other factions would prefer that a committee assume this role.[14]

The Maktabi will probably hold the reins as long as the IRP remains in power, but faced with a violent succession struggle, IRP factions may look for outside allies. The choice of such allies may have nothing to do with the ideological positions of the individual factions. The Soviets could exploit this to a limited extent, since, while the United States and the Soviet Union are both "Satans," the latter is less strongly condemned. This difference should not be overestimated, for Islamic leaders have few illusions about Soviet intentions. Any increase in Soviet influence, which is now at a fairly low level, would be unlikely to approach a satellitization of Iran. On the other hand, the anticommunist and anti-Maktabi sentiments of the two minority factions, particularly the Hojjatiyya, may also provide openings—although with great difficulty and danger—for the United States. Since the Soviet Union is in a better position to exploit factional rivalries, however, major instability in Iran is more likely to provide opportunities for Moscow than for Washington.

Another, non-IRP clerical group may be even more important as a potential Western ally. This group can be called the "traditionalist" clergy, including many senior ayatollahs who have never really accepted Khomeini's primacy or policies because of their impression that he has violated Shi'a Islamic traditions and because of his exclusion of high-ranking clerics and their followings from the new power structure. Many from the holy city of Mashhad in the northeast resent Qom's higher status. Leading figures in the traditionalist group include the ayatollahs Shirazi, Qomi, and Golpayagani and the ailing Shari'atmadari. Most of these men are old, and their influence is at present contained, but they could reemerge in the post-Khomeini era, and there are younger men with similar opinions. These men are likely to oppose Montazeri's succession, radical economic change, Soviet influence, and even clerical domination in the political realm itself. They might claim precedence in terms of religious authority over the Maktabi's men, and they are probably somewhat less hostile toward the United States. In a battle against IRP authority, these respected men could play a major role, perhaps in alliance with the armed forces.

Obviously, the military will play an important part in any power struggle that moves beyond IRP factional squabbles. But it must always be remembered that Iran now has two armies: the regular armed forces and the Revolutionary Guards. The former's advantage in any struggle should not be overrated. Many of the military officers now in command were men of relatively low rank under the shah and owe their elevation to the revolution. The purging of many shah-era officers, the indoctrination of enlisted men, and the placing of Islamic "political commissars" in units are all important constraints on the army. The patriotism manifested during the Iran-Iraq War also ties the military to the regime, despite officers' reluctance to cross the border into Iraq and to continue fighting for the total destruction of the Baghdad government. The genuine repulsion with which many current commanders view the use of the army against civilians in the 1978-79 revolution will also deter its entry into politics. If a power vacuum were to appear, however, the army could well become a contender and might be expected to side with non-IRP Islamic-oriented forces. While past U.S. training and the use of U.S. arms are important factors in their world view, the anti-Americanism of the last few years and the increasing employment of Soviet-made light weapons must also be taken into consideration.[15] An army-dominated regime might be an Iranian version of the Ba'th regimes of Syria and Iraq—a nationalist military dictatorship (in Islamic rather than Arab socialist clothing), either nonaligned or with a slight pro-U.S. or pro-Soviet tilt.

The Revolutionary Guards should not, however, be counted out. With its growth, improved training, and strategic distribution throughout the country, it is the Maktabi's praetorian guard. It also enjoys legitimacy from its association with Khomeini, while the army is still tainted by its association with the shah's era. It is improving on its past lack of discipline and training and is highly dedicated. Indeed, it might itself take power, alongside of or even overshadowing civilian clerical allies. The use of the Revolutionary Guards in so a political way would, however, arouse the jealousy and perhaps the competition of the regular military.

Future instability, then, is a major threat to Iran. It could lead to national disintegration and persuade some forces to seek Moscow's aid, producing an upsurge in Soviet influence or the establishment of a pro-Soviet client regime, even the potential for a Soviet invasion. These developments, however, are of low probability. More likely is a continuation of the current system for Khomeini's lifetime and then an attempt at a Maktabi-led extension of this system. Momentum alone will probably preserve this structure in the short run. Its survival in the medium term will depend on its ability to make internal compromises and to demonstrate policy flexibility on economic and foreign problems.

In addition to consolidating, legitimating, and centralizing its power, the Iranian government must deal with urgent economic problems and find some way to end the war with Iraq. Economic efforts are likely to lead to increasing oil production and to a cautious, selective development plan with an emphasis on self-sufficiency. Influence will go hand in hand with Tehran's choice of foreign partners for such measures.

Aware of this, the Iranians prefer smaller countries to the United States or the Soviet Union, but Western influence can be maintained through the involvement of European or Japanese firms. While Iran is more durable than Iraq in any war of attrition, the conflict's costs in lives and money are increasingly being felt at home. Just as it had to end the hostage crisis when its internal usefulness was exhausted, the Tehran regime may have to find the best way out of the war by persuading Khomeini or his successor to settle for something less than the stated Iranian demands. Monetary aid from Gulf oil-producing countries has been offered, without success, to this end. Internal change in Iraq could also provide an excuse for declaring victory and reaching a settlement.[16]

In the four years since the revolution, Iran's Islamic government has shown its ability to remain in power and demonstrated the seriousness with which it views nonalignment. Khomeini set out to break down traditional Iranian fears of omnipotent foreign great powers and to use his revolution as an example to encourage others to defy the United States and the Soviet Union. As Foreign Minister Ali Akbar Velayati explains this attitude, "Our revolution has presented the world with the new belief that one can fight but remain independent; one can fight against America without depending on the Soviet Union; and one can fight against those who possess modern weapons and advanced technology without submitting to another great power in order to receive weapons."[17]

Since Khomeini clearly saw the Iranian revolution as a model for imitation—in a way reminiscent of the French and Russian Revolutions—the Gulf Arab states have been very worried that they would be targets for fundamentalist subversion or even Iranian expansionism. Tehran's victories in its war with Iraq have sometimes turned this concern into something approaching panic.[18]

Nevertheless, the likelihood of a regional fundamentalist earthquake or a new Iranian empire is not great, although Arab anxiety is understandable in the light of hostile Iranian statements. Hojjat al-Eslam 'Ali Khamena'i, Iran's president, has called the rulers of oil-rich Arab states "greedy pigs that know nothing but satisfying their lust, sheiks who have spent their whole life plundering your wealth" and asserted, "We will destroy all the dwarfs if they continue to support falsehood against right. . . . All of you must raise the flag of the Islamic Revolution everywhere."[19] Tehran is especially angry about their support of Iraq's war effort and portrays them as U.S. pawns constantly plotting against it. Although Khomeini's Islamic and anti-Western ideology does appeal to some of the Gulf's poor Arab masses, those who see the revolution in terms of Iranian nationalism and Shi'ism are repelled. Consequently, the Islamic Republic cannot easily spread revolution abroad. The Gulf regimes are not democratic, but they have a strong position of legitimacy with their people. Oil wealth is often inequitably distributed, but the emirates have been able to disburse far more benefits with fewer social dislocations than Iran experienced under the shah.

Iran poses three types of threat to the Gulf Arab states:

1. Direct attack. Iranian planes could bomb Saudi oil fields within fifteen minutes of takeoff. The United States has supplied the AWACS airborne radar system to help guard against this possibility, but it provides only early warning, not protection. Such an attack would be costly for the Iranian regime because of possible reprisals against its own petroleum installations. Iran ships its own oil through the Gulf.[20]

2. Fundamentalist subversion. Iran produces propaganda, training, and aid for Gulf revolutionaries. The arrest of one such group in Bahrain in December 1981 and the discovery of arms caches set off a regional panic. Even without direct help, local fundamentalist opposition groups may conclude that if the Iranians could take power, so can they. Any upsurge in terrorism could destabilize and intimidate the Gulf Arab countries.[21] The period of greatest receptivity to such efforts, however, was the immediate aftermath of the revolution. Since then, the Gulf governments have had time to counter potential subversion with security measures and social and economic reforms. Saudi Arabia, for example, has moved to improve conditions for its own small Shi'ite minoriity, which comprises 40 to 60 percent of the oil-field workers. With high oil revenues relative to sparse population, the emirates have far more economic flexibility than did the shah, and their economic policies have been far more cautious. If necessary, these governments will take on an even greater Islamic coloration to dilute Iranian appeals. Further, most Saudis are strict Sunnis, religiously antagonistic to Shi'ism. Foreign workers, divided among themselves by language and culture, are not a major base for revolution; their primary interest is in making money and returning home.

3. Great-power politics. In more conventional political terms, Iran could use its size and strength to pressure the Gulf Arab states to adopt anti-American policies. Application of this leverage is a realistic possibility as the Islamic Revolution follows in the shah's foreign-policy footsteps, but it would probably push the Gulf Arab states closer to the United States. After a deadlocked Iran-Iraq War and Khomeini's passing, Iran's internal problems and exhaustion will probably lessen its capacity to mount an overseas offensive.

Washington is strongly committed to countries Iran perceives as enemies. Even after the Iran-Iraq War, hostility will likely continue; on this issue, Iranian nationalism and Iranian Islamic Revolutionism are in full agreement. While the demands of dealing with perceived Soviet expansionism impel the United States toward an attempt to rebuild relations with Iran, the demands of supporting Arab allies push it in the opposite direction. The two interests must be carefully balanced. Support for Arab allies must be tempered by the need to avoid pushing Iran toward Moscow, although the Soviet Union's own pro-Iraq tilt makes this eventuality less likely. Prudence dictates that the United States avoid entanglement on the Iraqi side of the war. Iran's size, location, population, vulnerability, and common border with the Soviet Union make it inherently the more important country from the United States's standpoint.

In fact, there is little the United States can do to help end the Iran-Iraq War. As long as Iraq's good behavior toward other Gulf Arab regimes (which it has frequently threatened in the past) is ensured and Iranian action against the emirates is limited, the continuation of the war at a relatively low level does not necessarily conflict with U.S. interests. The argument for more U.S. backing for Iraq to improve relations with both Baghdad and the other anti-Iran Arab states has a number of problems: Would Iraq really change its policy toward the United States and regional issues? What would Washington actually do for Baghdad, since it is unlikely that it would sell large amounts of arms or send troops to help the war effort there? How would Iran react to such a move? While the United States does not want to see an Islamic regime in Baghdad (relatively unlikely in any event), the survival of Iraqi President Saddam Hosain or his regime is not vital to U.S. interests. While hoping that Iraq will stand firm against Iran's offensives, the United States will have to focus its energies and resources on protecting Saudi Arabia, Kuwait, and the other Gulf states.

An IRP government steering a nonaligned course without any sharp increase in Soviet influence or in Iranian aggressiveness in the Gulf is the most likely scenario at least for the first portion of the coming decade. In this case, the United States should play a low-key role, awaiting opportunities, encouraging Western allies to be active, and strengthening Arab friends.

Different developments would call for different responses. A full-scale Soviet invasion of Iran, unlikely as it is, must be considered by defense planners. Such an invasion could well lead, unless under the clearest Iranian invitation, to World War III. The Rapid Deployment Force would likely function as a trip wire in such a case. It would be almost equally difficult to cope with an internal takeover by pro-Soviet elements. However, should unpatriotic IRP elements try such a sharp turn, it would alienate such wide sectors within the country that the United States would find many potential allies in opposing it.

Surprisingly, time may be on the U.S. side in some ways. The longer it takes for a major internal Iranian crisis to erupt, the more likely it is that Iran will have gotten over its bitterness toward the United States. At present, however, the Islamic Republic's survival and military victories convince Iranians that their break with Washington has not been so costly as to call for the rebuilding of relations. Every Iranian political figure knows that advocacy of a more friendly policy toward the United States would be instantly perceived by his colleagues as an act of treason.

While the United States has suffered a real loss in Iran's switch from friendly to neutral in the East-West conflict, this does not mean that a further move into the other camp is inevitable. Any major change for the better in U.S.-Iran relations will have to await a different regime in Tehran or the passage of many years.

Notes

1. *Iran Times*, January 24, 1983.
2. *New York Times*, November 5, 1982.
3. *Wall Street Journal*, April 26, 1982.
4. On the history of U.S.-Iran relations, see Barry Rubin, *Paved with Good Intentions* (New York: Oxford University Press, 1980); Yonah Alexander and Allan Nanes, eds., *The United States and Iran: A Documentary History* (Frederick, Md.: University Publications of America, 1980).
5. *New York Times*, November 19, 1982.
6. Interviews with U.S. government officials.
7. The problems of Gulf security are discussed extensively in the three-volume study, *Security in the Persian Gulf* (Montclair, N.J.: Allanheld, Osmun, 1981): vol. 1, Shahram Chubin, *Domestic Political Factors;* vol. 2, Robert Litwak, *Sources of Inter-State Conflict;* vol. 3, Avi Plascov, *Modernization, Political Development, and Stability.* See also Alvin Cottrell, ed., *The Persian Gulf States* (Baltimore: Johns Hopkins University Press, 1980).
8. On the clerical forces and domestic politics, see Shahrough Akhavi, *Religion and Politics in Contemporary Iran* (Albany: State University of New York Press, 1980); Michael Fischer, *Iran: From Religious Dispute to Revolution* (Cambridge, Mass.: Harvard University Press); Nikki Keddie, *Roots of Revolution: An Interpretive History of Modern Iran* (New Haven: Yale University Press, 1981); Nikki Keddie and Michael Bonine, eds., *Modern Iran: The Dialectics of Continuity and Change* (Albany: State University of New York Press, 1981).
9. On Iran's economy, see Bijan Mossavar-Rahmani, "Economic Implications for Iran and Iraq," in *Iran-Iraq War: Old Conflicts, New Weapons*, ed. Shirin Tahrir-Kheli (New York: Praeger, 1982); *Financial Times*, May 3, 1983; *Wall Street*

Journal, April 25, 1983; "Back to the Bazaar," *Middle East*, April 1983; *Washington Post*, April 10, 1983.

10. For analysis of the struggle for political power, see Sepehr Zabih, *Iran since the Revolution* (Baltimore: Johns Hopkins University Press, 1982), and Elaine Sciolino, "Iran's Durable Revolution," *Foreign Affairs*, Spring 1983, pp. 893–920.

11. On the Tuda's fall, see Jean Gueyras, "L'Iran en mal de normalisation," *Le Monde*, June 1–3, 1983.

12. On the Kurds, see Khomeini's statement, Tehran Radio, June 4, 1983, cited in Foreign Broadcast Information Service, South Asia (hereafter FBIS/SA), June 6, 1983, p. I1; Terry Povey, "Kurdish Headache for Baghdad and Tehran," *Middle East*, August 1983.

13. Interviews with U.S. journalists.

14. On the secession issue, see William Olson, "The Secession Crisis in Iran," *Washington Quarterly*, Summer 1983. On the factions and factional alignments of the clergy, see Shahrough Akhavi, "Clerical Politics in Iran since 1979," in Nikki R. Keddie and Eric Hooglund, eds., *The Iranian Revolution and the Islamic Republic* (Washington, D.C.: Middle East Institute and Woodrow Wilson Center, 1982). *Wall Street Journal*, December 1, 1982; Shaul Bakhash,"The Revolution Against Itself," *New York Review of Books*, November 18, 1982; John Renner, "Inside Iran," *Listener*, June 9, 1983. The IRP's Central Council's members are listed in *Jomhuri-ye Eslami*, May 16, 1983.

15. On officers' attitudes, see William Hickman, *Ravaged and Reborn: The Iranian Army* (Washington, D.C.: Brookings Institution, 1982). See also *Washington Post*, April 8, 1982; William Staudenmaier, "A Strategic Analysis," in Tahrir-Kheli, *Iran-Iraq War*; Clarence A. Robinson, "Iraq, Iran Acquiring Chinese-Built Fighters," *Aviation Week and Space Technology*, April 11, 1983; *Wall Street Journal*, March 8, April 26, and November 9, 1982; *New York Times*, August 24, 1983.

16. On Iraq's economic weakness, see "Fear of the Ayatollah Keeps Iraq in Business," *Economist*, September 3, 1983.

17. Tehran Radio, July 1, 1982, in FBIS/SA, July 7, 1982, p. I6.

18. On Arab attitudes toward the revolution, see Barry Rubin, "The Iranian Revolution and Gulf Instability," in Tahrir-Kheli, *Iran-Iraq War*; Adeed Dawisha, "Iran's Mullahs and the Arab Masses," *Washington Quarterly*, Summer 1983.

19. Tehran Radio, October 3, 1980, in FBIS/SA, October 3, 1980.

20. Velayati warned, according to *Kayhan International*, August 4, 1983, that if there was any obstruction to the export of Iranian oil, no other country would be able to transport its oil through the Gulf: "The leaders of the Islamic Iran will never allow the region to be unsafe for Iran only. . . ."

21. Bruce Maddy-Weizman, "Islam and Arabism: The Iran-Iraq War," *Washington Quarterly*, Autumn 1982.

ZALMAY KHALILZAD

Soviet Dilemmas in Khomeini's Iran

The spring 1983 banning of the pro-Soviet Tuda (Communist) party, the jailing of more than a thousand of its members including its leader, and the expulsion of eighteen Soviet diplomats from Tehran represent a significant setback for Soviet efforts to gain increased influence in Iran. This Iranian action was a high point of the hostility between the two countries, which had been increasing over the preceding year.

The case of Iran illustrates that domestic changes in developing countries do not always function as opportunities for Soviet gains as U.S. policy makers sometimes seem to fear. These changes can equally pose policy dilemmas for Moscow and constrain its gains. In Iran, Moscow's initial expectation of increased cooperation with the postshah government has gradually given way to a Soviet policy that mirrors Washington's. Both superpowers are worried about Iranian efforts to export their revolution and would like to contain them. Both Moscow and Washington are concerned about internal Iranian instability and careful to avoid pushing Iran toward closer ties with the other side.

The possibility of further changes in relations between Moscow and Tehran cannot be excluded, as these relations are essentially unstable. Some of these possible changes are of more than theoretical interest, as they could conceivably lead to dramatic changes in the balance of power in the region and in some extreme circumstances even to a superpower war. In this essay an attempt will be made to assess Moscow's initial policies toward the Islamic Republic, to examine the evolution of these relations and the failure of Soviet efforts to gain greater influence in Iran, and to identify the continuing relative Soviet advantages in Iran and the conditions that are likely to be conducive to dramatic changes in Iranian-Soviet relations.

Moscow and the Iranian Revolution

Soviet interest in Iran has been persistent and has included defensive and offensive considerations as well as political and economic ones. On

113

the defensive side, Iran could be a potential launching point for threats against the Soviets. Because certain religious and ethnic groups exist on both sides of their common border, Moscow is likely to be concerned that developments in Iran could affect its own rapidly growing Muslim population. From the offensive standpoint, Iran is pivotal for the region, and control of it would provide Moscow with a land presence along the Persian Gulf and the Arabian Sea contiguous to its own territory. Such a change would have a dramatic effect on the Soviet Union's international position, giving it considerable leverage against the West and making Western defense of the rest of the Gulf much more difficult. Moscow would also gain substantial economic benefits. The Soviets have already expressed interest in Iranian and Gulf oil resources, pointing out that they too might become increasingly dependent on oil from this region.[1]

As in the case of other contiguous states, in Iran too the Soviets have sought to replace Western influence with their own. However, they have pursued this goal while avoiding the risk of a serious confrontation with the United States. In areas where American stakes have been substantial and American ability to defend the region considerable, Moscow has pursued a cautious policy, promoting and exploiting opportunity. Moscow seems to have perceived the revolt against the shah as providing an opportunity for increasing its influence in Iran and the region. However, the overthrow of the shah under Islamic auspices was apparently as much of a surprise to Moscow as it had been to Washington. The Soviets, too, were conceptually unprepared for a revolt of this type. According to standard Soviet analysis, political movements led by Islamic ideology were essentially anachronistic and reactionary. After the Iranian revolt, several Soviet analysts sought to revise earlier views and to reconcile the Iranian development with orthodox Marxist-Leninist ideology,[2] but the events in Iran have continued to present explanatory dilemmas.[3]

After initial hesitation, Moscow in the fall of 1978 came out in support of the opposition to the shah. Either the Soviets believed that the fall of the shah was inevitable and wanted to be on the winning side or they preferred to encourage the emergence of a different regime or, more likely, a combination of the two. Despite substantial economic and other relations, Moscow obviously could not be pleased with the shah, a close ally of the United States whose regional policies were often inimical to Soviet wishes. Khomeini and his promise of nonalignment may have seemed a more desirable alternative. They may also have believed that the manifest hostility toward the United States of the opposition groups would lead them to seek closer ties with the other superpower. Finally, it is also possible that Soviet observers misjudged the situation. They may have believed the religious movement to be merely the vehicle for the "progressive" social forces and expected the figurehead Khomeini to give way to the left.

Once the shah had been overthrown, Moscow praised Iran's new regime, especially its decision to withdraw from CENTO and to remove U.S. monitoring posts. The Soviets expressed satisfaction with the damage that the Iranian revolt had done to the American security concept for this region. Under the pseudonym of Alexoi Petrov, which is attached to authoritative articles, *Pravda* acknowledged that the "fall of the shah had created cracks in the notorious strategic arc that the Americans had been building for decades close to the southern border of the Soviet Union."[4] Moscow sought to encourage the new government to deepen its break with Washington[5] and to reorient its economic and security relations.[6] Soviet analysts described the successful uprising as a positive development because of its "anti-imperialist" character[7] and even emphasized the positive role that traditional elements in society can play. According to one analyst, "Social progress in the East is unthinkable unless the vast body of traditional elements is involved in it."[8] Brezhnev and other leaders emphasized their desire for "good-neighborliness" between the two countries and for the strengthening of economic and security ties.[9] However, as early as 1979 other Soviet analysts saw Iranian developments as manifesting a counterrevolutionary trend that served the interests of the bourgeoisie and the professional middle class. This trend, it was argued, involved "Muslim figures" who "displayed a tendency to neutralize and to isolate left-wing forces."[10] These contradictory analyses illustrate at least a degree of Soviet ambivalence about Iran's Islamic Republic from the beginning.

Since the overthrow of the shah, the Soviet Union and its Iranian friends have emphasized several themes, although the relative weight put on some points has changed over time. One priority, as mentioned above, has been a continuous propaganda effort to encourage and intensify Iranian hostility to and dissociation from the United States and its allies. While the United States sought to absolve itself of any responsibility for Iran's internal conflicts, the Soviets were busy blaming them on Washington, which was charged with responsibility for "bomb explosions,"[11] for the Iran-Iraq War, and for preventing greater Iranian military victories by encouraging Arabs to join the war against Iran.[12] The Tuda party's National Voice of Iran (NVOI) broadcasts from Baku warned Iranians that U.S. forces were in the area as part of Washington's aggressive designs on Iran.[13] Recently, the Saudi refusal to accept Iranian demands to lower its oil production was blamed on Washington's "monopolist interests."[14]

Second, Moscow has tried to encourage the regime in Tehran to weaken the position of those regarded as hostile to the Soviet Union. Efforts have been made to identify anti-Soviet Iranian officials as agents of the "satanic" United States who should be "eliminated."[15] Moscow has also sought to encourage greater regime tolerance of and cooperation with pro-Soviet forces, especially the Tuda party, and encouraged the adoption of radical domestic economic policies.

Third, the Soviet Union has sought to discourage Iranian economic ties and cooperation with regional states friendly toward the West. The NVOI has declared that "friends of the United States cannot be friends of the Islamic Republic."[16] Moscow seems especially worried about recent improvements in Iran's economic relations with Turkey and Pakistan.[17] Both countries have been charged with plotting against Iran and with taking Iran back into CENTO through a "back door" of economic dependence.[18] Moscow has also sought to discourage friendly relations with China, perhaps fearing the emergence of security cooperation between the two countries.[19]

Fourth, the Soviet Union has tried to decrease Iranian hostility toward Soviet regional policies, especially its invasion of Afghanistan, while encouraging Iran to seek a better economic, political, and military relationship with the Soviet Union and its allies and friends. From the beginning, the Soviet Union has sought to present itself as the protector of the Iranian revolution and the supporter of the new regime. It moved quickly to offer aid to the new regime. In meetings with Khomeini and others, the Soviet envoy in Tehran reportedly offered Moscow's assistance in many areas.[20] Tehran was urged to "take advantage of these offers," and those opposing closer ties were attacked as counterrevolutionaries.[21] Apparently some economic and military exchange did result from these efforts (Iranian officials deny the purchase of any major weapons systems from Moscow because of unacceptable conditions attached to them, especially in regard to Afghanistan) but not to the extent that the Soviet Union may have desired.

The overthrow of the shah and ouster of the United States from Iran were major geostrategic gains for the Soviet Union. However, for the most part, as recent events indicate, Moscow's efforts to gain greater influence in Iran have not worked. Indeed, as we shall see, some of its heavy-handed tactics have been counterproductive. Tehran and Moscow have become increasingly unhappy about each other's policies. Why has Moscow failed so far in achieving its goals in Iran?

Problems in Soviet-Iranian Relations

Ideological hostility. A major impediment to greater Soviet influence in Iran has been the ideological hostility of the ruling elite toward the great powers. Although the United States has been the main target of criticism of the Islamic radicals, Moscow has not been forgotten. Already in 1964 Khomeini had said, "America is worse than Britain, Britain is worse than America. The Soviet Union is worse than both of them. They are all worse and more unclean than each other."[22]

The central document of the new regime commits Iran to the slogan "Neither East nor West." Principle 192 of Chapter 10 of the new constitution asserts Iran's nonalignment "with respect to the dominating powers." Principle 153 excludes the possibility of any type of agreement that allows a foreign power "to dominate the natural resources or the economic, cultural, military, and other affairs of the country." Khomeini personally has called on other nations to rebel against the superpowers.[23] The Islamic Republican Party (IRP) program has a similar tenor. It declares that "our revolution" will not be reconciled with any oppressive or domineering power and will pay "attention to the dangers that the Great Satan [i.e., the United States] and social imperialism pose to our revolution and our nation."[24]

Khomeini has attacked the Soviets specifically on many occasions. For example, in a speech on the occasion of the Persian New Year in March 1980, he warned his listeners: "Dear Friends! Be fully aware that the danger represented by the communist powers is no less than that of America."[25] Slogans of "Death to America" have at times been accompanied by chants of "Death to the Soviet Union" at national ceremonies and in the presence of government leaders.[26] Government-controlled broadcasting has presented unflattering reports[27] of Soviet involvement in various parts of the world. NVOI has attacked Iranian radio and television as the "mouthpiece of international capitalism" for its attacks on the Soviet Union.[28] It has also attacked Iranian leaders who place Moscow on "the same level" as the United States.[29]

Despite ideological hostility toward the Soviets, however, the Islamic government has entered into significant economic and security relations with them for pragmatic reasons, just as the shah did, though seeking not to become too dependent on its northern neighbor.

Fear of Soviet expansionism and intervention. Except for pro-Soviet leftists, Iranians have traditionally been apprehensive about Russian expansionism for historical reasons. In the nineteenth century, the Russians forced Iran to concede territory (in treaties such as those of Golestan in 1813 and Torkmanchai in 1828), and twice since the Russian Revolution Moscow has occupied Iranian territory (1920–21 and 1944–45). After the overthrow of the shah, both the modernists who dominated the Bazargan provisional government and the fundamentalists feared external interference in Iranian affairs. Bazargan warned both the Soviets and the Americans not to interfere, and the warning was repeated by Khomeini.[30] Moscow denied any involvement in Iran's internal affairs, but it provided the Tuda party with financial support and a "clandestine" radio station (NVOI). Many Tuda members returned to Iran after the shah's overthrow. With Soviet backing, Tuda strategy appears to have been to express support for the regime while encouraging the Maktabi fundamentalists to eliminate forces it regarded as hostile to the Soviets and as possible alternatives to the Khomeini regime. The Tuda supported the ouster of the Bazargan government, the removal of Bani-Sadr, the execution of Qotbzada, and the regime's attacks against the Mojahedin. Recently the object of attack has been the Hojjatiyya faction of the IRP, which is denounced as a "pseudoreligious" organization hiding behind the "Islamic mask" but in fact serving U.S. interests.[31] The Tuda sought to exploit the incipient division within the IRP in the hope that internal conflict would further narrow the regime's base, making it more vulnerable to Soviet and Tuda manipulation. Its aim was to "inherit the revolution"; it hoped that secular forces dissatisfied with other leftist groups and the regime would turn to it. Part of its strategy was infiltration of the military, the Revolutionary Guards, and the bureaucracy. After the Tuda was banned, several military officers, including the commander of the naval forces, were arrested and accused of working for the Communist party.

The Tuda's close identification with Moscow made it the object of much suspicion on the part of broad segments of the Iranian political elite. Initially the Khomeini government showed greater tolerance toward it. The Tuda's newspaper, *Mardom*, was allowed to be published when the papers of other groups had already been banned. Subsequently, the regime moved against the Tuda as well, closing its newspaper and purging some of its members from government and universities.[32] Early in 1983, Nur al-Din Kianuri and several other party leaders were jailed; finally the party was banned, and more than a thousand of its members were jailed later in the year. NVOI and Tuda supporters outside the country have rejected charges that it is "imperialist"-inspired. They claim that the Tuda has "protected the revolution" and has "not violated the constitution."[33] Jailed Tuda leaders have since admitted in public testimony to (1) working closely with the Soviet Union, (2) supplying political and military secrets to the Soviet Union, (3) supporting the Islamic Republic tactically while planning its overthrow, and (4) seeking more supporters in the military and better organization.[34] The circumstances under which these confessions were elicited must obviously be kept in mind in evaluating them. A clash between the IRP and the Tuda was inevitable because of their different attitudes on many issues and IRP desires for total control and elimination of rivals. Several other rival groups, including Westernized modernists, Islamic leftists (Mojahedin-e Khalq), and more radical leftists had already been attacked and weakened. The Tuda's turn had to come eventually.

Soviet tactics. Some of the Soviet tactics in seeking increased influence in Iran have been heavy-handed and counterproductive. One case illustrating this tendency is Moscow's ties with groups in ethnic minority areas hostile to the regime. As Bazargan's deputy 'Abbas Amir-Entezam complained to American embassy officials in Tehran in 1979, "Soviet overflights were a real problem." In one case, the government gave permission for overflights of Mazandaran at 21,000 feet. Instead, Soviet planes came at 4,000 feet and en route to the Persian Gulf dropped at least one large packet to the dissident Kurds. The Soviets had also made requests for Baluchistan overflights, which had not been approved.[35] Amir-Entezam also reported that his government had located and confiscated eight 50-watt transmitters placed at various locations by the Soviets to "broadcast subversive material."[36] As foreign minister, Qotbzada complained in August 1980, some two months after he had expelled a Soviet diplomat on charges of spying, that "substantial amounts of Russian arms not used by the armed forces of neighboring countries had been found in Kurdistan." He also accused Moscow of sending money and photographs of Iranian military positions to the Kurds.[37] Indeed, some Soviet statements concerning Iranian minorities have been menacing. For example, Hegdar Aligev, a Politburo member from Soviet Azerbaijan, is reported to have told journalists that he hoped the Soviet Union and Iranian Azerbaijanis would be united in the future. Another example of Soviet ties with minority groups is the fact that the Soviets criticized the banning of the Kurdish Democratic Party in 1979 and later a pro-Soviet faction emerged within it. Moscow has also maintained ties with Azerbaijan, without overtly encouraging its secession.[38]

In general, it appears that Moscow's policy toward Iranian ethnic groups has undergone several changes. Immediately after the shah's overthrow, Moscow apparently sought to strengthen ties with ethnic nationalists, especially in the Kurdish areas. Subsequently fearing that they might push the Iranian government toward the West, the Soviets encouraged their ethnic friends to follow a more moderate policy. The recent deterioration in relations between the two countries might lead Moscow to encourage greater ethnic opposition to the Tehran government.

Another Soviet tactic unpopular in Iran has been its refusal to accept Iranian renunciation of the "Treaty of Friendship" between the two countries signed in 1921. This treaty was signed under the pressure of Soviet occupation of parts of northern Iran. Articles 5 and 6 give Moscow the right to intervene in Iran if a third country threatens to attack the Soviet Union from Iran or if Iran becomes a base for "anti-Soviet aggression." The Soviets invoked this treaty when they invaded Iran in

1941 and have insisted on their right to send troops into Iran if they perceived a danger from an outside power operating through it. Under the shah, Moscow tried unsuccessfully to use it as an instrument to pressure Iran to forego military ties with the West. It also used it to warn Washington against intervention in 1978. Because of this treaty, Moscow assigns only what can be characterized as "limited sovereignty" to Iran. Not surprisingly, Iranians have several times sought to renounce it.

When Iran once again renounced this treaty after the overthrow of the shah, Moscow, as in the past, insisted on its validity. Moscow argues that this insistence indicates its commitment to Iranian independence; to the Iranians it is an indication of Moscow's expansionist designs on their country, particularly in the light of events in Afghanistan, where a similar treaty provided the pretext for the invasion. Qotbzada charged in 1980 that Moscow's refusal to recognize Iran's abrogation of the treaty indicated that it wanted to use the treaty "as a pretext to launch aggression and attacks against our country."[39]

Economic problems. In Paris, Khomeini had charged that while the United States was exploiting Iranian oil resources, the Soviet Union was exploiting Iranian natural gas. Because of strikes, Iranian natural gas exports had been disrupted during the upheaval against the shah's regime. When Iran began to sell gas again in April 1979, soon after the new regime was established, conflict between the two countries developed over what price Moscow ought to pay for it. The Iranians were pushing for a fivefold price increase, from $0.76 per thousand cubic feet to $3.80, the world market level.[40] Moscow's refusal to go higher than $2.66 led to a shutdown of shipments in March 1980. The Khomeini regime also cancelled the second Iran Natural Gas Trunkline, which was expected to be completed in 1981 and was to deliver more gas to the Soviets.[41] The Soviets had agreed to a complex arrangement by which they would have delivered gas to Western Europe in amounts equivalent to that received from Iran. Some of the transit charges against Iran would have been paid in the form of gas deliveries (3 million cubic meters of gas per year). Moscow tried hard to prevent the cancellation of the project, but the Iranians apparently wanted to avoid being too dependent on the Soviet Union. Recently they have been talking about shipping their natural gas to Western Europe through Turkey. Moscow has tried unsuccessfully to prevent improved economic relations between Tehran and Ankara. Because of the decline in gas exports to the Soviets, total Iranian exports to the Soviets have decreased. According to IMF data, Iranian exports to the Soviet Union declined from $64 million in 1978 to $33 million in 1981. However, as we shall see, imports from the Soviet Union and its allies have increased significantly.

Conflict over regional policies. Several regional issues have affected Iran's relations with the Soviet Union. One is the Soviet invasion of Afghanistan. Like the shah, the Khomeini regime had been concerned about the Marxist-Leninist regime in Afghanistan even before the invasion. The pro-Soviet regime in Kabul, adopting a policy parallel to Moscow's, expressed support for the Khomeini-led revolt against the shah even though it was being challenged by opponents some of whom had ideological preferences similar to Khomeini's. The Iranian government did not reciprocate, and relations between the two countries deteriorated. Even before the Soviet invasion, many Iranian fundamentalist, traditionalist, and modernist leaders had expressed opposition to the Soviet-dominated government in Kabul and warned Moscow against interference there.[42]

Despite their problems with the United States during the hostage crisis, Iranian leaders were vocal in their condemnation of the Soviet invasion of Afghanistan. Qotbzada characterized the invasion as "a hostile measure against not only the people of the country but all Moslems of the world."[43] Bani-Sadr charged Moscow with hostile designs against the entire region and demanded immediate and unconditional Soviet withdrawal.[44] Khomeini, too, has on many occasions condemned the Soviet invasion. For example, on March 21, 1980, he declared, "I vehemently condemn once more the savage occupation of Afghanistan by the aggressive plunderers of the East, and I hope that the noble Muslim people of Afghanistan will achieve victory and true independence as soon as possible and be delivered from the clutches of the so-called champions of the working class."[45]

Iran boycotted the Moscow Olympics and has taken a hard line against the Soviets in international meetings such as the Islamic Conference, the nonaligned meetings, and the UN General Assembly. The Iranian media often discuss the Afghan crisis and portray the Soviets as an aggressive imperialist power. The Iranian foreign minister refused to participate in UN-sponsored talks concerning Afghanistan in Geneva in the summer of 1982. The condemnation of the Soviet move has been a persistent theme in Iranian declarations, even after the eruption of the Iran-Iraq War further exacerbated Iran's conflict with the United States. However, while loud and persistent in its condemnation of the Soviet move, Tehran has been cautious in actual policy. It has not provided substantial assistance to the Afghan resistance groups. Its reported treatment of Afghan refugees, requiring special identity cards and sending them to fight against Iraq, for example, has caused resentment among Afghans.[46]

Soviet statements on Afghanistan to Iran, in contrast to those to Pakistan, rather than being threatening and harsh have contended that

Tehran has "misunderstood" Soviet motives. NVOI has sought to persuade Iranians that the Afghan partisans are counterrevolutionaries.[47] The Afghan partisans are also charged with collaboration with Israel and the United States, both unpopular in Khomeini's Iran.[48] Iranian official reporting on Afghanistan is characterized as "distorted."[49] NVOI has also called on Iran to return Afghan refugees to Afghanistan.[50] At times, Soviet-controlled broadcasts have attacked key IRP leaders for supporting the Afghan partisans.[51] Afghanistan is portrayed as a people's democracy with a legitimate government, and Iran is urged to seek immediate normalization of relations with Kabul.[52]

Another regional crisis affecting Soviet-Iran relations has been the Iran-Iraq War, which has been going on since September 22, 1980, and has posed major dilemmas for the Soviets. On one side is Iraq, a country that has a treaty of friendship with Moscow and is a major purchaser of Soviet arms. Relations between the two have been somewhat strained by the Soviet invasion of Afghanistan, the Ethiopia-Somalia dispute, Baghdad's treatment of the Iraqi Communist party, and the Iraqi-Syrian conflict. On the other side is strategically important Iran, where the Americans have suffered a major defeat and where Moscow is seeking greater influence. Moscow is likely to have feared that if it supported Iraq, Iran might move back toward the West. A failure to support Iraq, however, could lead to further deterioration of Soviet-Iraqi relations. Moscow must have been concerned about the Western response to the war, especially the possibility of greater American military presence in the region and increased security cooperation between some of the local states and Washington.

Moscow's official position was one of neutrality; in its public statements, it emphasized that the war should stop and that only "imperialists" would benefit from it. However, its actual policies favored Iran. Apparently, Moscow had decided that Iran was the more important country and that its potential gain or loss would lead to fundamental change in the geostrategic environment in the area. To demonstrate good will toward Iran it stopped arms shipments to Iraq, while maintaining economic ties. It offered to sell major weapons systems to Iran. It signed a treaty of friendship with Syria, Iraq's rival and Iran's ally. This policy brought only limited success. Iran apparently bought some arms from the Soviets and more from Soviet friends such as Libya, Syria, and North Korea. At the same time, however, it purchased American arms from the Israelis and others on the international illegal arms market, which is evidence of a very pragmatic attitude on the part of the Iranian leaders. Iran was unwilling to move very close to the Soviets.

As Iran began to do better in the war, Moscow changed its policy in a direction favorable to Iraq. This change in direction was perhaps a consequence of frustration with the lack of progress in relations with Iran, fear of a total loss of influence in Iraq, and the spread of Islamic fundamentalism. In fact, since 1982, containing the Iranian revolution has increasingly become an important Soviet goal. Iranians claim that Moscow fears the possible appeal of Islamic Republicanism among its own growing Muslim population. It has curtailed contact between Iranians and Soviet Central Asia and has canceled planned visits by Iranians to this region. It has resumed supplying major weapons systems to Iraq, and NVOI and Moscow's local friends attacked Iran's move into Iraqi territory in the spring and summer of 1982.[53] While opposing the spread of the Iranian revolution to Iraq, Moscow is likely to avoid actions that might push Iran toward security ties with the West. However, there may well be uncertainty in Moscow as to what Soviet actions short of direct military threat might lead to such a dramatic change in Iranian policy.

Iran's policies toward the region have not been entirely disagreeable to Moscow. Iran has opposed the presence of U.S. forces and facilities in the region, and countering U.S. efforts to reestablish a military presence in the region has been one of the most important Soviet concerns. Moscow fears that American forces might prevent internal and regional changes desired by the Soviets but unfavorable for Washington and might even be used to reestablish a position of influence in Iran. Besides, these forces bring American power to the southern flanks of the Soviet Union and challenge its potential hegemony over the region. The presence of American forces in the area increases the risk for the Soviets of any military moves they might make against the countries of the region. Moscow has tried to take advantage of local sensitivities with regard to foreign military presence in the region to promote opposition to U.S. efforts. Iran has followed a similar policy.

Moscow has supported the idea of turning the Indian Ocean (including the Arabian Sea) into a "zone of peace," excluding the naval forces of the great powers from the region. The Soviets have also called for an end to the dispatch of large naval formations to the region and to conducting large military exercises there and have opposed any increase in the number of Western-controlled bases.[54] Adoption of these measures would have several benefits for the Soviets. The Soviet forces that might move against Iran and surrounding areas are land-based in contiguous territories, either in the Soviet Union itself or in Afghanistan. Excluding the great powers from the waters of the area would further change the military balance against the West. To deal with the security problems of oil exports from the Gulf, Moscow has proposed a users' conference with Soviet participation to guarantee access to, and the flow of oil from, the area. The Soviets want to convince the Gulf states, Europe, and Japan that U.S. policies in the region will cause problems for the oil trade. They are offering an alternative security framework in which Moscow will have a role in determining Western oil supply.

Soviet Advantages in Iran

Despite the underlying problems in Soviet-Iranian relations and the recent setback, Moscow enjoys considerable advantages over the United States in dealing with Iran. A number of these have been present for some time, but their relative importance has increased because of changes in Iran's internal politics and external linkages. The revolution in Iran has changed the relative balance of interest and power in that country in favor of the Soviet Union and against the United States.

The most important factor favoring Moscow is Iran's geographic proximity. Traditionally this has been a double-edged sword. Contiguity to the Soviet Union and experience with its tendency toward border expansion have contributed to suspicion of Moscow and of its sympathizers within Iran. This fear in the past pushed Iran to seek close security relations with a distant counterbalancing power, the United States. On the other hand, contiguity insures the Soviet Union the advantages of sustained interest and easier military access. Since the shah's overthrow and Iran's break with the United States, the practical consequences of Iran's geographic contiguity have acquired greater importance. The decline of Iran's security capabilities has made it more vulnerable to such efforts as infiltration of Iranian territory from across the Soviet border. The existence of ethnically similar populations on both sides of their common border not only ensures Soviet interest in Iran but also provides Moscow with a large number of potential infiltrators to collect information and perhaps affect internal Iranian developments.

Another aspect of Moscow's proximity advantage is the substantial Soviet forces in military districts adjacent to Iran. These forces number some twenty divisions in various degrees of readiness and include airborne forces available for rapid deployment. Several more divisions could be brought to the Iranian border in a relatively short time. In some ways, the Soviet invasion of Afghanistan has further increased Soviet capabilities for coercing or, less likely, invading Iran. Soviet military involvement in Afghanistan could serve as a cover for preparatory steps to move against Iran. Deception has been a standard part of Moscow's invasion strategy. Soviet military preparations near Iran might well be presented as part of Moscow's efforts to reinforce troops in Afghanistan.

Moscow could use its superior relative capability to support sympathetic groups should they come to power and ask for Soviet assistance or to prevent the United States and others from intervening in Iran on the side of those sympathetic to the West in the event of escalated domestic conflict. The substantial Soviet military capability is likely to affect U.S. policies toward Iran. Washington may well be reluctant to move massively and directly in support of sympathetic groups or a friendly regime in Iran. Moscow, on the other hand, is likely to take substantial risks to prevent the emergence of a pro-West regime in Iran. The 1921 treaty could provide the legal rationalization for military intervention, especially if another power sent forces into Iran. Given Iran's strategic importance and Soviet proximity and capability advantages, U.S. interest in Iran in the near future is guaranteed and U.S. attempts to play on Iran's fear of the aggressive neighbor easily predictable. However, there is a danger that a greater Soviet capability advantage may in time bring about the tacit assignment of Iran to the Soviet sphere of influence.

Since the shah's overthrow, Moscow's relative stake in Iran has increased (although this may be changing because of the recent change in relations). The Soviets' fears that Iran under the control of an Islamic fundamentalist regime bent on exporting its revolution might affect their own rapidly growing Muslim population are believed by many Iranian officials to be considerable.

Another factor affecting relative Soviet interest in Iran is economics, and here the overthrow of the shah has had a mixed effect. Of course, American economic ties were undermined dramatically. Iran exported more than $4 billion worth of goods to the United States in 1978, and American nonmilitary exports to Iran were more than $4 billion. In 1977, 84 percent of Iranian exports and 84.8 percent of imports were with the Western industrialized countries. During the same period, the Soviet-bloc countries received 0.5 percent of Iran's exports and provided 3.7 percent of its imports. According to IMF data, Iranian exports have remained at the same level as before the shah's overthrow, but imports from the Soviet-bloc countries have increased. In 1980, imports from the Soviet-bloc countries formed 8.3 percent of Iran's total imports. The relative share for the Western industrialized countries was 67 percent. Iran has also become more dependent on the Soviets for imports and exports of its goods to other countries. Reportedly Iranian exports at the Jolfa railhead, on the Soviet border, between March and September of 1981 increased by 138 percent over those of the same period the year before. At the same time, imports through Iran's Caspian Sea ports showed an 84 percent increase in the first six months of 1981 over those of the same period during the previous year.[55] Recently, however, Iran has improved its economic relations with Japan, Turkey, China, Pakistan, and India.

There has also been a shift in Iran's purchase of military hardware in favor of the Soviets and their allies. While the shah purchased some military equipment from the Soviets (more than $1.5 billion), it was a small part of his total purchases. The current Iranian regime has refused Soviet "military assistance" but has purchased weapons from the Soviets and their allies. Given the dramatic decline in Western arms supply to Iran, the relative importance of arms from the Soviets and their friends (Eastern Europe, Libya, Syria, North Korea) has increased significantly.

Unlike Washington, Moscow continues to have a large embassy in Tehran and a large number of economic advisors in the country. It maintains cautious contact with several opposition groups, including ethnically based ones. For these reasons, it is possible that Moscow could be better informed on domestic Iranian developments than the United States.

Conditions Conducive to a Soviet Invasion

The circumstances under which Moscow might send its military forces into Iran are difficult to predict. Equally difficult to assess are the risks Moscow would find acceptable under what circumstances. At best it may be possible to identify the kinds of conditions that might be conducive to such a Soviet move, recognizing that surprises are always possible.

1. *Domestic Iranian developments.* In general, Soviet military operations against small neighboring countries are characterized by a low propensity for risk taking. Moscow uses indirect methods to extend its influence over such states and to reduce that of its opponents. Subsequently it uses direct methods, including massive force, to protect its gains, especially if the "correlation" of forces favors Moscow. It appears that the closer the relations of a small contiguous country to Moscow, the more likely it is that that country will be invaded by the Soviets. On the surface this invading of friendly countries appears paradoxical. In fact, however, it is indicative of Moscow's policy of gradual extension of its power and influence along its borders and its commitment to the irreversibility of gains made in these areas.

The changes in Iran, especially its break with the United States, have made it a more likely target of Soviet military intervention. However, given the established pattern of Soviet expansion, the Iranian situation has not yet evolved to the point at which such a move could be expected. The domestic political situation in Iran is characterized by suspicion, and American interest is still intense. Iran remains ideologically hostile. Despite the shift in relative interest in Moscow's favor, the region remains vital to the United States and its allies. Washington has threatened to use its own forces in defense of the region (the Carter Doctrine), and Moscow cannot be sure that an invasion of Iran would not lead to direct conflict with the United States, a conflict which might escalate both vertically and horizontally.

Should Iran move ideologically closer, going as far as the takeover of the state apparatus by pro-Soviet forces (an unlikely development in the foreseeable future but one that should not be entirely ruled out), Moscow's involvement in Iran would increase substantially in order to strengthen the regime and Soviet-Iranian ties. Such a regime would inevitably face serious domestic opposition from many political groups and would move closer to Moscow not only because of its ideological preferences but also to trap Moscow into supporting it against its opponents. The Soviets would be willing to provide assistance in order to avoid the perception of abandonment and in order to increase their influence in Iran and decrease that of others. Should the gains made be threatened, the Soviets would be more willing to intervene massively to protect them. Moscow might believe that under such circumstances the risks of intervention would decline to a tolerable level. Washington would be less likely to risk a war with the Soviet Union over Iran if the government in Tehran had moved close to the Soviets ideologically, if the Iranians had asked Moscow for help, and if the relative military balance favored Moscow. The move against the Tuda by the Tehran government, however, has reduced the possibility of a pro-Soviet takeover of the government in Iran in the foreseeable future.

2. *U.S. action.* Moscow might intervene militarily in Iran if it anticipated such a move by the United States. For the Soviets, the reestablishment of U.S. influence in Iran is among the least desirable of developments. It is very difficult to envisage circumstances under which Washington might intervene militarily in Iran, especially if no Soviet intervention had taken place. Although it is unlikely, one might speculate that internal conflicts in Iran could lead to the emergence of a pro-Western government. Such a regime would be likely to have many opponents, and Moscow might support some or all of them. Washington might become involved and might even intervene in support of such a regime; a Soviet counterresponse could lead to one of several possibilities. The Soviets have warned: "We shall intervene massively and immediately if the Americans get involved [in Iran]."[56] However, the possibility of a Soviet invasion might be reduced if a pro-Western government had substantial popular support and could consolidate without need for direct American intervention.

Another domestic development that might tempt Moscow to intervene would be the disintegration of the center in Iran and a splitting of the country into its several ethnic components, which include the Kurds and Azerbajanis next to Soviet territory. In 1945, the Soviets, while in Iran, established Soviet-oriented republics in these territories that collapsed as soon as the troops were withdrawn. If the center were to disintegrate, Moscow, perhaps on the invitation of some sympathetic local group or with the rationale of restoring law and order, might move into these areas to establish Soviet-oriented governments. A Soviet intervention in northern Iran might lead to a Western move against the south, and this could lead either to a de facto division of Iran into Russian-occupied north, central Iran, and Western-dominated south or to a conflict between the Soviets and the West for control of the country as a whole. While ethnic politics remains a threat to Iran's stability, this factor alone cannot lead to its "Balkanization." Even with the erosion of the capability of the government since the shah's overthrow, ethnic nationalists have not succeeded in escaping central control. Although there are many conflicts at the center, a total breakdown appears unlikely in the near future. A critical test for the regime's success at consolidation will, of course, be the aftermath of Khomeini's death. Whether his successor(s) will be able to do as well as Khomeini remains to be seen.

3. *Conflict in other theaters.* The Soviets might intervene in Iran if a conflict between Moscow and the West in an area vital to the Soviets was going badly for the Soviets. An invasion of Iran could be Moscow's horizontal escalation either to compensate for its losses elsewhere or to place itself in a strong bargaining position in the other theater. Moscow might use this option if it became convinced that the military balance unambiguously favored it in Iran and the West might not escalate. However, of the scenarios considered, I regard this one as the least credible. It is difficult to envisage an American military move against vital Soviet interests in, for example, Eastern Europe. A war in Central Europe appears extremely unlikely, but should one occur there would be grave danger of vertical escalation.

Historical Soviet strategic behavior toward contiguous states, while clearly the most important predictor, cannot lead to certainty regarding expected Soviet action against Iran. As Ezer Weizman noted after the October 1973 war, "There are two popular folk sayings that are as fatal to military concepts as they are to political ones: 'There is no wisdom like experience,' and 'History repeats itself' . . . for the man of experience who relies on the stability of history, wisdom becomes a broken reed."[57] It is a truism that surprise is always possible, and Moscow has proven capable of taking unexpected action (such as the placing of missiles in Cuba).

Prospects

Despite problems in Soviet-Iranian relations, the revolution in Iran represented a major opportunity for the Soviets. Because of internal instabilities in Iran, relations between the two countries are susceptible of further significant change. Moscow is likely to use both positive and negative incentives to discourage Iran from moving toward the West and to encourage it to persist in its hostility to the United States and its independent strategy in the region. Like Washington, Moscow faces the dilemma of avoiding pushing Iran toward its rival while containing Iranian efforts to export its revolution. In Moscow's hierarchy of preferences, the return of a pro-Western government in Iran with security ties to the West is clearly one of the least desirable of developments. In conformity with their policy of defending their gains, the Soviets might even take drastic measures to prevent this from occurring. At the same time, we have seen Moscow oppose Iranian efforts to spread Iranian-style Islamic Republicanism in the region. It is likely to persist in using indirect methods to gain more influence in Iran and arming Iraq to defeat Iranian regional policies. Despite the ban on the Tuda and the expulsion of eighteen Soviet diplomats, Moscow is likely to continue to offer Iran increased economic, political, and cultural ties and favorable terms on the exchange of its goods with socialist countries. It is unlikely, however, to abandon its clandestine support for sympathetic groups that might eventually become powerful enough to take over the state.

Whether the Soviet strategy will succeed depends on several factors, many of which are not under Moscow's control. The most important is Iran's domestic politics. Although the Islamic regime has made considerable strides in consolidating its power, it continues to face many opponents, and there are serious conflicts within the IRP. It is difficult to categorize the internal conflicts accurately, especially on the issue of relations with the Soviets. In general it has been assumed (by the Soviets, among others) that the Hojjatiyya faction is more hostile to the Soviets than the others. If so, the recent turn in Soviet-Iranian relations may reflect a shift in the domestic configuration of power in favor of this group. While it appears that all the IRP factions are committed to nonalignment and distance from the Soviets, some might be more willing to accept expanded economic and military relations, and this means that the evolution of the power struggle between the various IRP factions could further affect Soviet-Iranian ties. Internal IRP conflicts may well intensify after Khomeini dies. Khomeini has dominated Iran's political scene since 1979 and is not openly challenged by any of the IRP factions.

In the event of a radical change in Iran's domestic politics, such as the overthrow of the Islamic Republic, relations between Moscow and Tehran would obviously depend on the character of the new regime. Among those involved in the opposition to the current regime, there are groups both more hostile and more friendly toward the Soviets than the current leaders.

Moscow's actions will also be affected by its calculations of Western capabilities and responses. The higher it perceives the Western stake in Iran to be and the greater it considers Western ability to retaliate against a Soviet threat to those interests, the more likely it is that Moscow will avoid using massive direct means to bring about important changes in Iran. Therefore the Soviet challenge to the West in Iran necessitates the development of a strategy that prevents further fundamental changes in both the balance of interest and the balance of power in Iran in favor of the Soviet Union. The only safe prediction seems to be that we are unlikely to have seen the last of Iranian upheavals and that Iran is likely to be one of the main testing grounds for superpower rivalry in the coming decade.

Notes

1. *Tass*, January 29, 1980.

2. Georgy Kim, "Ideological Struggle in Developing Countries," *Journal of International Affairs*, April 1980.

3. Y. Primakov, "Dialectic of Social Development and Ideological Struggle: Islam and Social Development Processes in Foreign Oriental Countries" (in Russian), *Voprosy Filosofii*, no. 5 (August 11, 1980); Alexandr Bovin, *Vedelya*, September 3–9, 1979.

4. December 31, 1979, in U.S. Department of Commerce, Foreign Broadcast Information Service (hereafter FBIS), Soviet Union, December 30, 1979, pp. D7–10.

5. In an April 4, 1979, *Pravda* article, Moscow claimed that "during the Iranian peoples' struggle against the monarchy, the USSR resolutely sided with the Iranian revolution and did everything to prevent outside interference in Iran's affairs and block plans for armed intervention against the revolution."

6. FBIS, Soviet Union, July 24, 1979, p. H1.

7. P. Demchenko, "Krusheniye absolyutizma," *Kommunist*, no. 3 (February 1979), p. 83. See also his "Iran: Stanovleniye respubliki," *Kommunist*, no. 9 (June 1979), p. 116.

8. Kim, "Ideological Struggle in Developing Countries," pp. 65–75.

9. There were several reports of Soviet offers to sell arms to Iran (*Times* [London], October 6, 1980; *Baltimore Sun*, August 23, 1980).

10. Primakov, "Dialectic," *op. cit.*; see also Bovin, in *Vedelya*.

11. NVOI, "Another Dreadful Crime by Agents of World-Devouring America," FBIS, South Asia Series (hereafter SAS), 82-037, February 24, 1982.

12. NVOI, "Washington's Satanic Policy," FBIS/SAS, 82-029, February 11, 1982.

13. NVOI, "Reagan's Hypocrisies," FBIS/SAS, 82-034.

14. FBIS/SAS, 82-093, May 13, 1982.

15. NVOI, "Dismiss the Liberals and Other Dregs from Sensitive Government Organizations," FBIS/SAS, 82-036, February 23, 1982.

16. FBIS/SAS, 82-091, May 11, 1982.

17. NVOI, "Being in Harmony with Ziaul Haq's Regime is Beneath the Dignity of Our Islamic Republic," FBIS/SAS, 82-097, May 1982.

18. FBIS/SAS, 82-096, May 18, 1982.

19. FBIS/SAS, 82-103, May 27, 1982.

20. 'Abbas Amir-Entezam reported the Soviet offers to the Americans (From Embassy in Tehran to the Secretary of State, October 9, 1979, no. 7950 [Secret]; also see no. 10977/1, October 15, 1979).

21. NVOI, "Justice Seekers Must Unite in a Single Rank," FBIS/SAS, 82-028, February 10, 1982. See also FBIS/SAS, 82-039, February 26, 1982, and 82-103, May 27, 1982.

22. Algar, *Islam and Revolution: The Writings and Declarations of Imam Khomeini* p. 185.

23. Speech, February 11, 1980.

24. IRP, *Mavaze'-e Ma*, p. 84.

25. Algar, *Islam and Revolution*, p. 285.

26. NVOI, "A Provocative Attack at the Esteglal Hotel," FBIS/SAS, 82-025, February 5, 1982. See also FBIS/SAS, April 6, 1982.

27. Pro-Soviet groups complained about this; see, for example, NVOI, "Dismiss the Liberals."

28. FBIS/SAS, April 13, 1982. In another broadcast it is attacked as a "mouthpiece of Western and SAVAKist interest" (FBIS/SAS, 82-039, February 26, 1982).

29. FBIS/SAS, 82-196, October 8, 1982.

30. *Financial Times*, June 13, 1979.

31. NVOI, "The Mask of U.S.-made Associations Must Be Ripped Off," FBIS/SAS, 82-096, May 18, 1982.

32. In a February 20, 1982, broadcast, NVOI complained that some Tuda students had been expelled from the university (FBIS/SAS, 82-036, February 23, 1982). A later statement complained further about the "purges" of a large number of "true revolutionaries" from Iran's educational institutions (FBIS/SAS, 82-076, April 20, 1982).

33. See *Rah-e Tuda* (a publication of Tuda supporters abroad, published in Frankfurt), no. 29 (Bahman 29, 1361); see also the open letter from 'Ali Khavari, member of the political council and the chairman of the Central Committee of Tuda, to Ayatollah Montazeri.

34. *Kayhan* (air mail edition), no. 520 (May 11, 1983), pp. 6–7. Not surprisingly, Moscow has denied the Tuda's Soviet connection, calling it "completely unfounded and baseless." In an article on May 6, 1983, *Pravda* called Tehran's action similar to those taken by reactionary and proimperialist regimes "in order to

smear the honorable and independent relations between the communist parties and the Soviet Communist party" (*Kayhan International,* May 9, 1983, p. 2). In a subsequent article *Pravda* accused the Iranian authorities of "using medieval tortures to extract confessions from the arrested leaders of the Tuda (Communist) party." Moscow argues that the "admissions" by Tuda leaders have "no foundation and nothing in common with reality" (*International Herald Tribune,* May 25, 1983, p. 2).

35. John Stemple's report after conversations with Amir-Entezam (From the Secretary of State to the Tehran Embassy, no. 3941, August 1979).

36. Ibid.

37. Qotbzada's message of August 11, 1980, to the Soviet foreign minister, circulated by the Muslim Student Association of the United States and Canada (P.O. Box 6322, Albany, Calif. 94706). Recently, the Iranians have disclosed that documents captured at the American embassy in Tehran indicate that Kurdish Democratic Party leaders had traveled to Moscow to obtain assistance in September 1979 (*Kayhan International,* June 2, 1983, p. 2).

38. Bakinskii Rabochii, October 9, 1981, JPRS, no. 79606, p. 31, cited by Muriel Atkin, "The Islamic Republic and the Soviet Union," in *The Iranian Revolution and the Islamic Republic,* p. 146.

39. Qotbzada's message of August 11, 1980.

40. Alvin Rubenstein, "The Soviet Union and Iran under Khomeini," *Journal of International Affairs,* Autumn 1981, p. 613.

41. *New York Times,* July 19, 1979.

42. *Financial Times,* June 13, 1979; *Dawn* (Karachi), September 20, 1979.

43. *Middle East,* April 1982, p. 18.

44. Ibid.

45. Algar, *Islam and Revolution,* p. 287.

46. Some Iranian opposition sources have accused the Khomeini regime of turning over Afghan refugees to the Soviet-installed government in Kabul (FBIS/ SAS, May 19, 1982).

47. FBIS/SAS, 82-197, September 15, 1979.

48. Ibid.

49. NVOI, "The Afghan Problem: An Excuse to Divert Public Opinion," FBIS/SAS, 82-175, September 9, 1982.

50. FBIS/SAS, 82-169, August 31, 1982.

51. FBIS/SAS, 82-166, August 26, 1982.

52. NVOI, "The People Are Defending the Democratic Government of Afghanistan," FBIS/SAS, 82-155, August 11, 1982. See also FBIS/SAS, 82-116, June 16, 1982.

53. FBIS/SAS, 82-110, June 8, 1982, and 82-123, June 25, 1982. "Continuation of the War Is But the Extension of the Enemy's External Policy," FBIS/SAS, 82-160, August 18, 1982. See also FBIS/SAS, 82-138, July 10, 1982.

54. Speech by Andrei Gromyko to the 37th session of the UN General Assembly, October 1, 1982.

55. International Monetary Fund, *Directions of Trade 1982* (Washington, D.C., 1983), pp. 987, 908.

56. *Middle East,* October 1982, p. 31.

57. Ezer Weizman, *On Eagles' Wings* (New York: Macmillan, 1976), p. 209.

RICHARD COTTAM

Iran's Perception
of the Superpowers

In the years since World War II there has been increasing recognition
of the importance of understanding how different peoples view each
other. Many students of international relations in particular are concerned
with discovering how foreign-policy decision makers define the international environment within which they must operate. The approach
may have particular utility for understanding contemporary Iranian
foreign policy—a foreign policy that seems to be in vital respects outside
any of the patterns we have come to recognize in the postwar period.
How does Khomeini view the international system, and how do the
major world actors view Khomeini?

Understandably, students of perception, like others in the international
relations field, have been preoccupied with the Soviet-American conflict.
That conflict, called the "cold war," has given general definition to
world politics for the past two generations. In imagery terms, the cold
war has served as a metaphor so remarkably descriptive that even
students of perception forget that it is in fact only a metaphor. Gamson
and Modigliani many years ago presented strong evidence that the
prevailing view of the United States in the Soviet Union and that of
the Soviet Union in the United States were mirror images.[1] Each country
tended to see the other as what Ralph White and others refer to as the
"diabolical enemy"[2]—ineluctably aggressive and evil in intent, monolithic
in decisional structure, rational in decisional style to the point of being
able to orchestrate highly elaborate conspiracies, and dependent for its
power advantage on superior will and determination.[3] In the scholarly
world, there has even been a willingness to agree that Soviet and
American decision makers have mirror images of each other without
drawing the obvious conclusion that, if so, both are wrong. The diabolical-
enemy image is a consequence of a perceived terrible threat from another
state capable of inflicting great damage. It is not the image held by, for
example, a Hitler of his intended victims. Hitler's image of France,
Britain, and the United States was one of an enervated, degenerate

133

people unable to muster the will to mobilize their admittedly great resources to resist his plans for domination. Were the Soviet Union or the United States similarly motivated, it would, it follows, see the other as degenerate, not diabolical. Whatever the logic of this, the evidence is strong that both American and Soviet decision makers concerned with Iran see their adversaries as engaged in elaborate conspiracies to bring revolutionary Iran into their camp, just as the mirror-image theory would predict.

American decision makers concerned with the Middle East had to reconcile three discrete objectives, each representing extremely strong foreign-policy interests: containing the Soviet Union, maintaining the flow of oil and later petrodollars to the United States and its allies, and preserving the security of the state of Israel. Over the years, the American definition of the situation in the Middle East came to reflect a reconciliation in world-view terms of these objectives. The policy formula came to be one of establishing a close ally/mentor relationship with Middle Eastern regimes that limited their hostility to Israel largely to the rhetorical level, that were anticommunist, and that modernized—sometimes with rapid growth rates—in a tightly controlled manner. Since many of the favored regimes were oil producers that saw their economic and political destinies as closely tied to those of the United States, all three objectives were happily realized. In the American view, the cooperating regimes were coded as "moderate," "responsible," "pro-Western" governments dedicated to the principles of the free world. Their opponents were viewed as "radical," "agitating," and the witting or unwitting surrogates of the Soviet Union. Leading moderate responsibles were the kings of Morocco, Jordan, and Saudi Arabia, President Bourguiba, and the sultans and emirs of the Arabian Peninsula. Of special importance were President Sadat of Egypt and Mohammad Reza Pahlavi of Iran. For a brief moment in 1977-78, with the Camp David formula developing, American policy seemed extraordinarily successful. The pro-Soviet states, Algeria, Libya, and Syria, were largely isolated, and there were signs that Iraq would follow Egypt in leaving the Soviet camp. Had it not been for the inexplicable growth of revolutionary fervor in the shah's Iran, the achievement of all three of the American objectives would appear to have been assured.

As might have been expected, according to the American view, the Soviet Union's embrace of "radical," "agitating" regimes was warm and seemingly generous. The People's Democratic Republic of Yemen possibly could claim a particular preference, but Soviet diplomatic support for Algeria, Libya, Syria, and Iraq was strong, and these states were coded by the Soviets as "progressive" and "peace-loving." There were, however, striking anomalies in Soviet behavior. The Soviet Union's acquiescence in its rude expulsion from Egypt, the most important of Arab states, was difficult to explain in diabolical-enemy terms. How could the Soviet Union be so accepting of the extraordinary success of its great enemy, and in its own backyard? Nor were the basically friendly, cooperative relations the Soviets had with the shah of Iran any easier to understand. Yet the fact is that Soviet expression of alarm at the American efforts to support the faltering shah became serious only in October and November of 1978—and by then the shah had passed the point of no return. This Soviet behavior is anomalous, however, only in terms of the diabolical-enemy image. That image is in fact a stereotype, an ideal type. There are individuals, and President Reagan appears to be one of them, whose view of the Soviet Union approximates the stereotype, but there are many others who see a Soviet Union that is complex in motivation and decisional structure and no more capable of orchestrating an elaborate conspiracy than our own ponderous bureaucracy.

Similarly, Soviet behavior in the Middle East appears to reflect a view of the United States that is midway between the simple stereotype and a rich, complex picture. For anyone holding the diabolical-enemy image of the United States, the acquiescence in the sudden replacement in Iran of a regime considered by many America's important ally/surrogate with a regime venomously hostile to the United States is difficult to explain. It was the good fortune of the revolutionary regime in Iran that it came into existence at a time in which the view of reality associated with the cold war was showing signs of atrophy.

Ayatollah Khomeini had his own world view and his own metaphor—the oppressed and the oppressors—to describe the essence of conflict in his world. Furthermore, since he believed that he was the instrument of a divine plan and must lead a movement toward the resolution of that conflict favorable to the oppressed, his metaphor was destined for even greater reification than was the cold-war metaphor. The cold war, after all, was a human, not a divine, pattern. According to Khomeini's view, the United States and the Soviet Union were the leading oppressor states of the world, and, although they could be dealt with differently tactically, both must be negative targets of Iranian foreign policy.

The Khomeini world view did not immediately prevail in revolutionary Iran. There were many signs that the government led by Khomeini's first appointee as premier, Mahdi Bazargan, would follow the traditional policy of Iranian governments of balancing the strongest external powers. Given the perceived division of the Middle East into pro-American and pro-Soviet camps, Iran could be expected to move sharply away from the pro-American friends of the shah but not so far as to associate fully with pro-Soviet regimes. The balancing process would thus adapt to cold-war-generated alliance patterns and in effect operate within the familiar cold-war context. But one year later Iran was engaged in a policy of humiliation of one of the great oppressors and was in the forefront of the Islamic states condemning the other great oppressor for its invasion of Afghanistan. Even more startling, it was getting away with both policies.

Four years later, in 1984, the operating Iranian world view is still Khomeini's. It is a world of oppressed and oppressors, and Khomeini's Islamic Republic is attempting to provide leadership for or at least to demonstrate the path to be followed by the oppressed peoples of the world. Khomeini's Iran therefore does not fall into the easily recognizable even though somewhat ambiguous category of nonaligned states. It is actively hostile to both superpowers and sees its mission as liberating the oppressed peoples from their domination. However, since it emerged from a revolution that overthrew the shah, a man universally regarded in revolutionary Iran as an agent of the United States, its treatment of the two oppressors could not be entirely symmetrical. Khomeini put it very well in a recent statement: "the arrogant world powers and hegemonists are all the same to us. However, the United States, because of the untold harm and blows it inflicted on us before and after the revolution, is the enemy facing us and nearer to us."[4]

Given their strikingly different world views, the governments of Iran, the United States, and the Soviet Union are certain to misread each other's foreign policy. It is possible, however, by looking in some detail at the Iranian world view, to anticipate some of the patterns of misunderstandings and the likely consequences of these misunderstandings. To do so we need to flesh out the Iranian world view and to describe the Iranian view of American and Soviet friends and allies and of states that are trying to be nonaligned.

America's allies among what the Khomeini government thinks of as the oppressor nations are treated somewhat differentially. Israel and Zionism are, of course, in a class by themselves. Not only are they central agents of the oppressor world, but they covet and occupy land that is holy to Islam. The liberation of Jerusalem must be the culminating act of the war against imperialist oppression in the Middle East. Indeed, the umbrella term for the offensive designed first to drive Iraqi troops from Iran, second to provide Iraq with an Islamic government, and third to move in to aid the Palestinians directly is "Operation Jerusalem." Zionism is the ubiquitous and seemingly omnipotent local agent of the imperialism of the Western capitalist oppressor.

A second oppressor, seen as an American ally, is treated with an opprobrium second only to that reserved for Israel—South Africa. Cutting off oil sales to South Africa was a policy favored by virtually the entire opposition to the shah, including Shapur Bakhtiar, but the symbolic role of South Africa and white Rhodesia for Khomeini and his supporters is exceptionally important. Khomeini's role as an instrument of the deliverance of oppressed peoples is a universal one. Africa and Latin America are particular victims of oppression, and the settler state of South Africa is entirely comparable to the settler state of Israel as a partner in America's overall hegemonic plan. Hojjat al-Eslam Faker has summarized the regime's views of these two lesser oppressors very well:

> Those who wish to bar the way to the export of our revolution should know that as long as Israel exists in the Middle East and as long as South Africa exists in Africa, our revolution is exportable. Let them strive to extirpate Israel and South Africa. The groundwork for the export of our Islamic Revolution is constituted by the injustices and bloodletting perpetrated by Israel in the region. When Israel is uprooted, then one can say that our revolution was exported.[5]

European allies of the United States are frequently classified among the oppressors. France in particular, because of its special relationship with Iraq and its playing host to the largest Iranian expatriate community, is most frequently coupled with the United States. Britain also is on occasion scathingly denounced.[6] West Germany and Italy are less frequent targets. Indeed, for the rest of Western Europe there is an attitude close to one of live and let live. The old preeminence of Britain as central actor in behind-the-scenes domination of Iran, first directly and later as the brains behind American activity, is a perception now largely confined to the opponents of Khomeini. For Khomeini and his followers, American preeminence among Western states is unchallenged.

It is hardly surprising, therefore, that those Middle Eastern regimes perceived by the American government as "moderate responsibles" are generally regarded in Iran as American clients. Khomeini frequently lists "Hosni, Hasan, Hosain, Nomairi" as "criminals of history" who must depend on America for their survival.[7] In the Arabian Peninsula, with the striking exception of the People's Democratic Republic of Yemen, all of the regimes are classified as reactionary regimes "who associated their interests with the United States and other imperialist countries."[8]

How should revolutionary Iran deal with such regimes? Both the statements of Iranian leaders and Iranian policy suggest that they are seen in the context of an overwhelming struggle with the United States. American policy, as the Iranians see it, is one of imposing and maintaining its guardianship over these regimes. Iranian policy quite simply is to eliminate that guardianship. As Hojjat al-Eslam Hashemi Rafsanjani recently put it, "We do not see Saddam as our main enemy. The United States was trying to create a gendarme in the region. It wanted to make

Saddam a guardian for the protection of Kuwait, Qatar, Dubai, Bahrain, Saudi Arabia and others. It wanted to remove the danger from Israel."[9] The Iran-Iraq War and the Israeli invasion of Lebanon, hence, are part of the same struggle. Imperialist control of the area is the objective, and Iraq's attack on Iran, Israel's ceaseless assault on the Palestinians, and Hosni Mobarak's subtle efforts to continue the policy of his predecessor in producing regional acceptance of that control are all aspects of the general strategy. Iran's response is to some degree tactically flexible, but there has been in three years no real deviation from basic strategic goals.

Flexibility is most apparent in Iran's dealings with Turkey and Pakistan. In his important foreign policy statement at Friday prayer on February 25, 1983, Rafsanjani made clear his view of Turkey and Pakistan as functionally allies of the oppressor world.[10] However, Iran has been sufficiently close to Turkey and Pakistan to draw the ire of the Soviet Union. On pragmatic grounds, this policy is easily defended. Turkey and Pakistan are major regional powers, and, given their close relations with the United States and given the Iranian assumption that Iraq's attack on Iran was a manifestation of American policy, the relative neutrality of Turkey and Pakistan regarding the Iran-Iraq War could be seen as a major diplomatic achievement. Furthermore, Turkey is a natural staging ground for Iranian so-called counterrevolutionaries wishing to infiltrate Iran. Halting or at least reducing Turkish cooperation with Iranian exiles, therefore, is an obvious Iranian objective and one that appears to have been achieved.

Overall, however, the Iranian hostility toward the United States embraces not only the American oppressor, but its lesser-power associates as well. Thus the Iranian view bears a striking resemblance to that held by, for example, the leaders of the People's Democratic Republic of Yemen and indeed to the view manifest in the Soviet press and radio. It must be more than a little confusing to the Soviet Union and its allies, then, that the Iranian government persists in viewing the Soviet Union too as an oppressor and hegemonist state. The statement of Khomeini quoted earlier indicates that the asymmetry in hostility is a function of the perceived proximity of the American threat. Iranian statements and policy seem entirely congruent with that view. Formal diplomatic ties with the Soviet Union are maintained. Soviet advisors are in Iran in significant numbers, and trade with Iran is now above prerevolutionary levels.[11] But the arrest of Tuda party leader Nur al-din Kianuri and the expulsion of a number of Soviet diplomats in the spring of 1983 was accompanied by Iranian statements to the effect that the Tuda party is an arm of Soviet political and intelligence activity in Iran. Prime Minister Mir-Hosain Musavi went farther: "The Tuda Party has been the oldest communist party in Iran which from the very beginning backed the Soviet Union's policies and ideology. They are widely blamed for laying the grounds for the U.S.-backed coup in 1953 by creating agitation and disturbances under the premiership of Mohammad Mosaddeq."[12] Implications of de facto Soviet-American collusion in perpetuating control over the oppressed are to be found throughout the remarks by Iranian leaders concerning world affairs.[13] Sometimes, though, especially regarding the war in Iraq, assertions of collusion are explicit. In his Friday sermon on February 4, 1983, Faker said, "Those people in the East who used to peddle socialism and those in the West who used to babble about liberty and equality are joining hands and standing against these barefooted oppressed people who have risen for their own salvation and independence and are delivering blows and aiding foes of this revolution. These two heads of imperialism are now knotted together in Iraq."[14]

Iran's view of the Soviet Union and policy toward it were expressed with unusual clarity in its response to the short-lived Brezhnev proposal concerning the Persian Gulf area made in New Delhi in December 1980. The plan called for a joint Soviet-American, East-West agreement to refrain from establishing bases in the area, arming the area, or restricting trade or the free flow of oil in the area. The American government rejected it out of hand. In contrast, Iran, though skeptical, was willing to explore:

> In any case, the proposal of the Soviet leader for the countries of the Middle East is a positive proposal in itself. However, it should be seen whether this plan is part of a propaganda campaign to regain Soviet credibility in the region, whether it is a well-meaning proposal for the interests of the Muslim masses of the region, or whether it is another propaganda campaign. . . . In this connection, the Soviet Union, to demonstrate its good will concerning the recent proposal, can put an end to the occupation of Afghanistan and leave its destiny to the Muslim people of that country. In addition to that, it should dismantle its bases in the region. In connection with the Iran-Iraq war, it should formally announce its neutrality and reaffirm that it does not sell arms to Iraq.[15]

On his return from the nonaligned conference in New Delhi in March 1983, Musavi was interviewed by Tehran radio. The question was as revealing of Iranian views as the answer:

> [Question] The Resolution passed by the conference did not raise the question of Soviet aggression against Afghanistan and only condemned the policies of the United States, especially in the Middle East region. From whom does this conservative approach originate?

[Answer] This conservative approach originates from the weakness of the Third World countries when faced with the oppressive powers of the world, on the one hand, and the lack of uniformity in the Non-aligned Conference on the other.

Musavi went on to point out that there were at the conference such allies of the United States as Jordan and Morocco and also a leftist contingent. He then remarked that the most important thing was "the prestige that our system gained and which is concomitant of the revolutionary fervor of our people and our nation and stems from our stance vis-à-vis the Afghan issue. None of the speeches was as articulate and lucid, none of the stances so clear on the issue as that of our country."[16]

Indeed, the remark of Khomeini quoted earlier—that Iran is opposed to both "hegemonic" powers but faces the most immediate threat from the United States and thus is most concerned with dealing with that threat—is entirely consistent with Iranian policy. The Soviet Union's invasion of Afghanistan, its continuing arms sales to Iraq, and the tepid quality of its help to the Arabs when Israel invaded Lebanon are the primary subjects of Iranian negative remarks concerning the Soviets. On the other hand, expressions of gratitude to the Soviet Union for opposing American designs in the area, a constant theme of the Arab left, are never found in Iranian statements. The Soviet Union is treated consistently as part of the oppressor world, and, whatever its struggles and conflicts with other states in that world, it is depicted as committed to a continuing oppression of the deprived countries. The appearance of a major challenge from the oppressed in the form of the Islamic Revolution in Iran did not generate from the Soviets a hostility parallel to that from the United States, but, as the Soviet Union's actions in Afghanistan and Iraq demonstrate, it is part of an anti-Islamic conspiracy.[17]

However, whereas the Iranian view of America's friends and allies in the Third World is unambiguously negative, the view of Soviet friends is often friendly. The Afghan regime is seen as simply Soviet-imposed, but other close Soviet friends, such as Cuba and Angola, are treated as honorable, even exemplary members of the community of the oppressed. To be sure, as the statement of the prime minister quoted above indicates, the Iranian government is fully conscious of the close relationships of many of its friends with the Soviet Union, but it appears to adopt an understanding attitude toward what it describes as weakness. Still, there is here a major problem for regime perceptions. As he sees it, Khomeini is playing a divinely inspired role in leading the oppressed world against the oppressors and at the same time leading an Islamic revival. These are not necessarily harmonious goals. Having purged his own secular liberal nationalists, Khomeini nevertheless must embrace secular nationalists in other parts of the Third World, including the Islamic world. Thus Cuba, militantly secular, militantly anti-American, yet dependent economically on the other great oppressor, is embraced warmly. Nicaragua, the El Salvador rebels, and Namibia's SWAPO are supported with great enthusiasm even though they are also, directly or indirectly, the beneficiaries of Soviet help.

The problem becomes even more serious as one moves into the Arab world. There Iran's great friends are Syria, Libya, Algeria, the Palestine Liberation Organization, and the PDRY—all to one degree or another secular and nationalist. Furthermore, Syria in particular is confronted with an exceedingly serious challenge from Sunni fundamentalist opponents, especially the Ikhwani. Since Khomeini is consistent in his verbal treatment of his movement as Islamic and not simply Shi'a, this Syrian opposition should pose a dilemma for him. However, when the Syrian government and the Ikhwani had a desperately serious confrontation in Hama in 1982, Iran did not hesitate to side with Asad. The statement issued by the Foreign Ministry revealed a detailed knowledge of the personalities involved in the Syrian Ikhwani, and this suggests more than a passing interest in that organization. In Foreign Minister Velayati's eyes the Ikhwani was functionally if not directly cooperating with Zionism and imperialism by challenging Asad at this critical moment in time. The condemnation of the Ikhwani was unreserved and hence revealed no sign of its being the result of a difficult decision. Thus the observer cannot know whether to assess this as another of several manifestations of pragmatism or as a reflection of some serious intersectarian conflict. The suspicion is inevitable that Shi'a Iran prefers the Syrian regime because of its ties with Shi'a-related Alavis.

The above picture reflects some pragmatic tendencies in Iranian policy and also some inherent contradictions, but all in all it is a highly integrated and remarkably consistent world view. Grounded as it is in a belief in divine inspiration and articulated by one of the world's truly charismatic leaders, the world view appears to be accepted unquestioningly by regime supporters. It is given expression by many individuals, often in elaborate form, but in general outline there appears to be as little variance in this expression as one sees in verbalizations from the Soviet Union or the People's Republic of China. This seems to represent more an internalization of a fairly simple general picture than a manifestation of totalitarian control. In explaining the consistency it is well to keep in mind the attribution of divine inspiration. According to a recent Khomeini statement,

It is hoped that the divine promise concerning assistance for the oppressed people will be implemented in the near future, that the powerful hand of Almighty God will be extended as soon as possible in the deprived nations, and that the same divine transformation which has taken place in the Iranian nation will also be manifested in all the nations and groups with the will of Almighty God, so that the criminal's power over the oppressed people of the world may be eliminated, and so that the wronged people may achieve their lost rights. . . . The beloved nation and the fighting forces have felt repeatedly during the revolution and this war that, were it not for divine assistance and for His special blessings, we would have never possessed the strength to withstand a satanic regime armed to the teeth, which was dependent upon world powers. However, because the nation, as a result of a divine transformation, staged an Islamic revolution based on spirituality, it succeeded in destroying that great power of the region. In this unequal war, despite all the weapons and unlimited assistance of the East, the West and the region to Iraq, it succeeded in achieving so many amazing successes for Islam and Iran.[18]

The cold-war-associated world views of the United States and the Soviet Union are also, in their extreme expression, highly integrated views. And since the Reagan administration, unlike the Carter administration, manifests little variance in its definition of the situation, there is certain to be a curious intersection of the two world views. In part, Iran's stance appeared to be recognizable to those holding a cold-war view. The Third World allies of Iran were substantially the same states that Americans with a diabolical-enemy view of the Soviet Union regarded as Soviet surrogates, and thus the suspicion was natural that Iran, too, was close to the Soviets. But Iran's tough stance on Afghanistan and unforgiving picture of the Soviet Union as a major oppressor power were incongruent with this view. Given these mixed signals, the American response seems to be one of withheld judgment. Unfavorable remarks about Iran are frequently made, suspicions are voiced of the extent of Soviet infiltration, and America's Gulf friends are sympathized with, but Iran unconnected with the Soviet Union is not terribly threatening, and reflecting this view the American response is at a low intensity level.

For the student of perception, the Soviet response to this Iranian perspective is far more interesting. Those preparing the script for the National Voice of Iran, a clandestine radio operating from Baku, are obviously thoroughly familiar with the Iranian world view and seek to adapt that view to their purposes. Confronted with a persisting anti-Soviet policy and recently the arrest of leading Tuda activists, the NVOI attempts to manipulate Iranian attitudes to discredit the Hojjatiyya faction of the current Iranian leadership—a faction thought to be more anti-Soviet, more conservative, and more probazaar than the followers of the line of the Imam. An example of the NVOI line is the following:

> Dear Compatriots: The great satan is preparing new plots against the Iranian people and our glorious revolution, whose fourth anniversary we are approaching. As you are aware, all the counterrevolutionary groups operating in France and Egypt against the Islamic Republic of Iran are supported financially by the bloodsucking U.S. imperialists. They spend millions of dollars to equip counterrevolutionary groups with the weapons of the imperialists. These groups, which are basically in Egypt, are given military training by U.S. military experts or experts affiliated with the CIA.[19]
>
> We know the Americans never concealed their support and praise for the liberals and their provisional government, the Bazargans, the Bani-Sadrs, the Entezams, the Yazdis, the Qotbzadas, the Shari'atmaderis, the Muslim People's Party, the Paikaris, and other counterrevolutionary mini-groups, particularly the CIA-affiliated hojjatis.[20]

Here in full bloom is the American diabolical enemy with its orchestrated conspiracies tacked onto the Iranian world view. Evidence for NVOI and Radio Moscow of the CIA's success is seen in the anti-Afghan policy of the government. It is also seen in the friendly relations of Iran with two of America's puppet regimes, Turkey and Pakistan. But for Americans who have the diabolical-enemy view of the Soviet Union, Iranian policy raises parallel suspicions. Iranian anti-American attitudes and Iranian policy toward Israel are clear and explicit manifestations of cooperation with friends of the Soviet Union. So are the frequent cultural and diplomatic exchanges of Iran with Angola, Cuba, and Nicaragua.

Still, the most characteristic feature of both Soviet and American policy toward Iran is a lack of excitement. The intersection of Iranian policy and Iranian imagery with Soviet and American policies appears to be such that neither superpower perceives an immediate intense threat associated with Iran. The Soviet Union is engaged in efforts overtly and covertly to establish friendly relations with Iran and to dissociate itself from the oppressor image. The United States seems largely unconcerned. Thus for the time being the international system—the arena of great-power interaction—is far less the source of disturbances to regional interactions than the recipient of them.

It follows that the analyst seeking to uncover the central dynamics associated with Iranian foreign policy should look at a lower level of activity, especially the Iran-Iraq War. The war, according to the Iranian view, originates with the oppressors, particularly the United States. Thus Rafsanjani says, "Since the United States failed in stopping the Islamic

Revolution in Iran . . . it decided to launch various plots to eliminate it such as coup plots, separation of Iranian provinces, and finally it imposed a war on the Iranian nation for which they found no better country in the Iranian neighbors except Iraq."[21] Khomeini broadens the charge: "since the beginning of the Islamic movement in Iran, especially since the great Iranian revolution, all the great powers have opposed the revolution with all their might. They have created impediments, launched military attacks, and invited the enemies of Islam to launch military attacks against some regions of the beloved Islamic country, only because of the offense of being Islamic."[22]

It follows that since the Iranian movement is in accord with a divine plan and Iran was attacked by the government of an Islamic state, the attacker is an instrument of an evil force and cannot be compromised with. Rather, the perpetrators must be punished. Hence all mediation efforts which fail to accommodate to the obvious logic of this point are doomed to failure, and the war persists. By another logic, one that Iran's good secular nationalist friends such as Algeria adhere to, the war is a senseless squandering of lives and resources and of benefit only to Zionism and imperialism. But Algeria, Syria, Libya, and the PLO seem to understand the world-view premises on which Iran's policy is based. Syria, Libya, and at least part of the PLO seem willing to pay the price of a valued Iranian alliance. This decision is made less difficult because of their hostility to Saddam Hosain. Yet all three Arab regimes continually lament the terrible price to Arab unity that the persisting conflict exacts. The Soviet Union echoes this lament but, like its Arab friends, apparently feels powerless to alter an Iranian view which has such solid grounding. The Iranian definition of the situation, it follows, is already one of the major determinants of regional political developments. Since the region is quite possibly the most dangerous of confrontational areas for the Soviet Union and the United States, it follows as well that Iranian policy, based on its unique and peculiar world view, is likely to have a serious effect on superpower relations. Simply put, the superpowers have lost control of the dynamics of the situation, and Iranian policy is a major factor in determining those dynamics.

To illustrate the potential dangers of the situation one need only turn to recent expressions of Iranian policy toward the Gulf states. Again Rafsanjani has been coldly explicit:

Today my Arabic sermon contains an ultimatum to other Arab countries that have supported Iraq. . . . What we want to say to the reactionary countries which have supported Baghdad is: You have provided it with a great deal of help. You have provided it with a lot of money, equipment, transportation, and port facilities. All these can be forgiven by us. We will seize the real culprit.

If the countries of the region do not sully themselves with this servitude to America and if they do not want to become a means of imposing a new government upon the people of Iraq, they can live with us in peace and security. They can be confident that neither now or any other time has the Islamic Republic any intention of engaging in aggression and violation against any country, especially neighboring countries. For us, only Israel is tyrannical and usurping by nature, and this is what we have announced and made clear.[23]

The newspaper *Sobh-e Azadagan* wrote on February 20, 1983,

So the reactionary regimes who associated their interests with the United States and the other imperialist countries have to be aware that these deeds of theirs will bring harm to their countries and their peoples. They must go back to the lap of Islam, abandon the 'Aflaqist regime in Baghdad, and stop squandering the wealth of their peoples since the fate that awaits Saddam is similar to the fates of the buried shah, of Sadat, of Bashir al-Jumayil, and of the other agents in the region.[24]

Iranian imagery is sui generis. It contains elements that are both familiar and confounding to those holding the more familiar images associated with the cold-war era—the Soviet and American diabolical-enemy images and the colonial image that defines the situation for secular nationalist regimes in the Middle East. The Iranian reality view and the foreign policy associated with it appear to Americans, Soviets, and secular-minded Middle Easterns as otherworldly. But, because neither the Americans nor the Soviets see Iran as tending toward or actively associating with the other, no strong policy toward Iran has crystallized in either government. The result is a superpower passivity toward Iran— a passivity that Khomeini and his supporters attribute to divine will. This attribution in turn allows the Iranian government a wildly exaggerated view of its own capability. Throughout history, governments have claimed to be the beneficiaries of divine favor in their interstate conflicts. The Iranian government, however, carries such a claim to the point of including divine favor in its capability calculus, and this allows Iranians to believe they are capable of defeating the two superpowers acting in collusion with Iraq. Furthermore, the Iranians appear to believe that they have the capability to challenge and defeat Israel and to liberate Palestine. The warnings to Arab allies of Iraq indicate that the Iranian government has contemplated with at least some seriousness attacking these states as well. Jordan, standing as it does between Iran and Palestine, is identified as an obstacle in the path of the liberators of

Jerusalem as long as the regime in power is that of King Hosain. Presumably Jordan, like Iraq, must accept an Islamic regime if the promise to liberate Jerusalem is to be fulfilled.

For a brief period, when Iraqi forces were being expelled from Iranian territory, some credibility was granted in the United States to Iranian claims to be a regional superpower. There was at that time a flurry of concern for American friends in the Arabian Peninsula. But as the Iran-Iraq War moved into stalemate, interest in Iran waned. Nevertheless, the American reaction in this period is a good predictor of the probable American response were the Saddam Hosain regime in Iraq to be replaced by a pro-Khomeini Islamic republic. Given the coincidence of the Iranian and Soviet imagery of the Arab world, emerging Iranian policy toward Arabs in all likelihood would appear in American eyes to be closely parallel to Soviet policy. The conclusion that Iran was becoming a Soviet surrogate would almost certainly follow, and confrontation would be difficult to avoid. On the other hand, were the Iranians, following the persecution of the Tuda party and the expulsion of Soviet diplomats, to focus primary attention on liberating Afghanistan, the Soviets could see Iran as becoming an American surrogate. Indeed, any number of dangerous scenarios with some plausibility can be constructed. All that can be predicted with real confidence, however, is that, owing to strongly divergent world views, Iran and the superpowers will badly misinterpret each other's foreign policy.

Notes

1. William Gamson and Andre Modigliani, *Untangling the Cold War* (Boston: Little, Brown, 1971).

2. Ralph White, *Nobody Wanted War: Misperception in Vietnam and Other Wars* (Garden City, N.Y.: Anchor, 1970). See also David Finlay, Ole Holsti, and Richard Fagen, *Enemies in Politics* (Chicago: Rand McNally, 1967).

3. For an explication of the components of stereotypes, see Richard Cottam, *Foreign Policy Motivation* (Pittsburgh: University of Pittsburgh Press, 1977).

4. Foreign Broadcast Information Service, South Asia (hereafter FBIS/SA), February 10, 1983, p. 14.

5. FBIS/SA, February 8, 1983, p. 17.

6. For example, see FBIS/SA, December 17, 1980.

7. FBIS/SA, February 15, 1983, Speech to the Nation of February 11.

8. FBIS/SA, February 23, 1983, p. 13.

9. FBIS/SA, February 28, 1983, p. 11.

10. Ibid.

11. *Iran Times*, April 1, 1983.

12. FBIS/SA, February 8, 1983, p. 16.

13. FBIS/SA, February 28, 1983, p. I1. Rafsanjani made this point in his major foreign policy statement.
14. FBIS/SA, February 8, 1983, p. I7.
15. FBIS/SA, December 15, 1980, pp. I21–23.
16. FBIS/SA, March 15, 1983, pp. I4–5.
17. FBIS/SA, February 9, 1983, pp. I9–10, Speech of February 4.
18. FBIS/SA, February 15, 1983, pp. I1–2, Speech of February 11.
19. FBIS/SA, February 9, 1983, pp. I4–5.
20. FBIS/SA, February 25, 1983, p. I8.
21. FBIS/SA, February 9, 1983, p. I1.
22. FBIS/SA, February 14, 1983, p. I1.
23. FBIS/SA, February 9, 1983, p. I11.
24. FBIS/SA, February 23, 1983, p. I3.

Appendix

These photographs are reproduced with the permission of Susan R. Kinsey of Long Island University and Youssef M. Ibrahim of the *Wall Street Journal*. The translations and annotations were done by Kinsey, Ibrahim, and Ervand Abrahamian of Baruch College, The City University of New York.

"Yesterday. Today. (Tomorrow)?" This poster, distributed by the Writers' Association in the spring of 1979, when the clerical authorities were starting to crack down on the secular forces that had fought the shah, symbolizes the bewildered and wilting flower of freedom wedged between the past, with its terror of U.S. imperialism, and the unknown future.

"For Today." This poster, distributed by the Writers' Association, commemorates the massacre of students at the University of Tehran in October 1978.

"Long Live Iran." This poster, distributed by the Writers' Association, portrays the political prisoners executed by the Pahlavi regime.

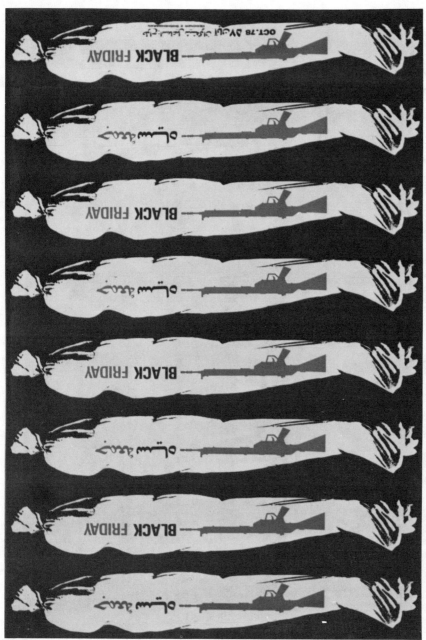

"Black Friday." This poster, distributed by the Writers' Association, commemorates the Zhala Square massacre.

"Black Friday." A poster commemorating the Zhala Square massacre.

Mosaddeq. This poster, distributed by the Writers' Association in February 1979, pays tribute to Dr. Mosaddeq, the prime minister who nationalized the oil industry in 1951 and was overthrown by a royalist coup in 1953.

"March 1979." This poster, distributed by the Writers' Association in March 1979, shows two guerrilla fighters killed by the Pahlavi regime and expresses concern about the future at a time when the Islamic Republic had started to crack down on its secular allies.

"May Day." May Day 1979 was celebrated with large rallies in the main industrial centers of Iran. This poster was distributed by left-wing unions.

"Iranian Universities Are the Bases of U.S. Imperialism." This poster, distributed by the religious Reconstruction Crusade, calls for a "cultural revolution" in the universities. This cultural revolution began in 1980, when the anticlerical forces—particularly the Mojahedin and the Feda'iyyin—came close to gaining control of the universities.

"The March to Protest Zionist News Networks." This poster was distributed by the Islamic Republican party. The Quranic inscription (*top left*) reads: "Oh believer, if a sinner brings you any news verify it."

Portrait of Ayatollah Khomeini. In the past, Shi'is in Iran—unlike Shi'is and Sunnis in the Arab world—referred to religious leaders as ayatollahs and reserved the title of Imam for the founding fathers of Shi'ism. During the Islamic Revolutuion of 1978-79, the Iranian public, in recognition of Khomeini's charismatic role, began to refer to him as Imam.

"Today Islam is in Danger." Khomeini, without his turban, is surrounded by admirers. The inscriptions are quotations from Khomeini warning that the United States, the USSR, and Britain threaten Iran and exhorting all groups to unite against foreign dangers.

Khomeini exhorting the people to overthrow the Pahlavi regime.

Khomeini and land reform. This poster, distributed in 1979-80 by the Reconstruction Crusade organized by the Islamic Republic to help the peasantry and the urban poor, quotes Khomeini as saying: "If the laws of Islam are put into effect, nobody will have large landholdings."

Khomeini, the man of the people. This religious poster shows Khomeini surrounded by the people—each figure depicts a particular occupational group,
including peasants, workers, and intellectuals. It clearly shows the influence of
the art of Russian "Socialist Realism."

Khomeini in contemplation by moonlight.

Khomeini, martyrdom, and the budding of the new.

Khomeini with the Holy Quran. This religious poster depicts two
critical scenes from the revolution: (1) The massacre of hundreds
of youngsters by the army in Zhala Square in Tehran on Friday,
September 8, 1978. This massacre has gone down in history as
Black Friday. (2) The rally of some two million in Tehran on
December 10, 1978, calling for the establishment of an Islamic
republic. The rally was held around a huge archway built by the
shah to celebrate the 2,500th anniversary of the monarchy. The
inscription in heavy lettering above Khomeini declares "God Is
Great." The inscription to the left reads in Arabic and Persian:
"Count not those who were slain in God's way as dead, but rather
living with their Lord, by Him provided."

A portrait of Ayatollah Khomeini.

Khomeini, the man of peace. This religious poster portrays Khomeini as a symbol of serenity surrounded by cherubs, the dove of peace, flowers, and a serpent-like monster that will attack the forces of evil. This poster, like many other religious posters in Iran, clearly shows the influence of the religious art of the Italian Baroque.

The shah in flight. This religious poster depicts the shah escaping from Iran, which has been transformed into an angry and powerful bird. The inscription at the top left reads: "The lowest among you will become the highest, and the highest among you the lowest." This Islamic concept is similar to the Christian idea that the meek will inherit the earth.

Youth. A schoolboy in contemplation beside the grave of a compatriot martyred in the revolution.

A war poster. This poster, depicting a scene from the Iran-Iraq War, exhorts the union of the Iranian people, the Revolutionary Guards, and the armed forces against foreign aggression.

Contributors

Shahrough Akhavi, Associate Professor of Government and International Studies, University of South Carolina; author of *Religion and Politics in Contemporary Iran: Clergy-State Relations in the Pahlavi Period.*

Mangol Bayat, Research Associate, Center for Middle East Studies, Harvard University; author of *Mysticism and Dissent: Socio-Religious Thought in Qajar Iran.*

Richard Cottam, Professor of Political Science, University of Pittsburgh; author of *Nationalism in Iran.*

William L. Hanaway, Jr., Chairman, Department of Oriental Studies, Professor of Persian, University of Pennsylvania; author of *The Pre-Safavid Persian Inscriptions of Khurasan I.*

Farhad Kazemi, Associate Professor of Political Science, Director of the Hagop Kevorkian Center for Near Eastern Studies, New York University; author of *Poverty and Revolution in Iran: The Migrant Poor, Urban Marginality, and Politics.*

Nikki R. Keddie, Professor of History, University of California, Los Angeles; author of *Roots of Revolution: An Interpretive History of Modern Iran.*

Zalmay Khalilzad, Assistant Professor of Political Science, Columbia University; coauthor, with Cheryl Benard, of *The Government of God: Iran's Islamic Republic.*

William B. Quandt, Senior Fellow, Brookings Institution; author of *Saudi Arabia in the 1980s: Foreign Policy, Security, and Oil.*

Barry M. Rosen, Assistant to the President, Brooklyn College, The City University of New York; coauthor, with Barbara Rosen and George Feifer, of *The Destined Hour.*

Barry Rubin, Senior Fellow, Center for Strategic and International Studies, Georgetown University; author of *Paved with Good Intentions: The American Experience and Iran.*

Jiman Tagavi, Assistant Professor of Political Science, Brooklyn College, The City University of New York.

173

Index